CW01066868

COSTIN
CONTRACTS

by

John Callaghan

A Directory of Social Change publication

COSTING FOR CONTRACTS

By John Callaghan

First published by the Directory of Social Change with the National Council for Voluntary Organisations, with financial assistance from the Allied Dunbar Charitable Trust.

ISBN 0 907164 81 1
Typeset by Joan Margolith and Jane Wood
Printed in Britain by Biddles of Guildford

Directory of Social Change, Radius Works, Back Lane, London NW3 1HL. Tel. 071-284 4364

National Council for Voluntary Organisations, 26 Bedford Square, London WC1B 3HU. Tel. 071-636 4066
(*Address from 1st June 1992*: Regents Wharf, 8 All Saints Street, London N1 9RL. Tel. 071-713 6161

Contents

Acknowledgements

Many people have contributed directly and indirectly to this book. I would particularly like to thank **Luke FitzHerbert** and **Jo Habib** for their encouragement and guidance. Other help has come from **Geoff Hill; Kate Sayer; Martin Jones; Peter Gallant; Steve Western;** and **Diana Woodhead.**

I have borrowed heavily from the section on VAT in a companion volume in the Contract Culture series "Getting Ready For Contracts" by **Richard Macfarlane** and **Sandy Adirondack.** I am also grateful to the **Social Services Inspectorate** and the **Association of Metropolitan Authorities** for permission to reproduce material from their publications.

Lastly I must thank Brenda, Jenny and Lucy, who have borne most of the indirect costs of writing this book.

Part I
INTRODUCTION

Chapter 1

Introduction

This book is primarily intended to help people in voluntary organisations – staff, volunteers, management committee members – to prepare realistic costings for services which are to be funded through contracts, service level agreements, or performance linked grant aid. I hope it will also help officers and members in purchasing authorities and funding organisations to understand better the very different financial world inhabited by the voluntary sector.

This is not a book for accountants. You don't need any previous costing or accounting experience to use this book. If you have, it should help you consolidate and make better use of that experience.

The book is also intended to equip the reader to reach their own conclusions about the suitability and viability of taking on a contract. I have tried to show readers how to make their own assessment of the complex relationship between the volume, quality and funding of the services their organisation provides.

Financial management, like other aspects of management, is a means, not an end. Voluntary organisations need management that is capable of responding positively to changing circumstances and new appreciations of clients' needs. This book does not seek to turn managers, staff or voluntary workers into accountants; but it does try to show that accountancy skills can and should be used to ensure that scarce resources are deployed to meet the highest priority needs, and where they are most effective.

The book is divided into five parts:

The *first* introductory section shows how you and your organisation can tackle the job of costing for contracts; and gives an overview of the costing process. A separate chapter explains the framework for defining and understanding what costs are.

The *second part* lists the items you may have to cost, and explains how to find out what they will cost. One chapter examines what you need to count when costing staff and volunteers. The next looks at premises, equipment and other assets. It includes an explanation of depreciation. That is followed by a chapter on administration, management and other hidden or indirect costs, and a short chapter on VAT. The last chapter in this part looks at the cost of quality and equal opportunities, and monitoring and evaluation.

The *third part* shows how to put that information into a budget, produce a cash flow analysis and calculate unit costs. It also looks at forecasting over several years, and at relating several contracts to each other, and to the rest of your organisation's activities.

The *fourth part* looks at how costings can be used at three different stages – deciding to take on a contract or not, pricing and negotiation, and in the management of a contract – and works through examples for each.

The *fifth part* contains guidance on checking your sums, and using computers.

Getting costing organised

Costing is not difficult. Anybody can do it, provided you are prepared to take care over details. You do need to be organised and systematic in working things out and you do need to use common sense in interpreting the figures you produce. Costing certainly gets a lot easier the more you do it.

In many voluntary organisations there are real difficulties for people without experience or training in costing to exercise real control over cost-based decisions. On the other hand there are few areas in which a voluntary management committee may wish to act which do not have cost implications. Organisations trying to maintain maximum participation by volunteers, staff or users in their affairs face particular problems. There are steps you can take to diminish the problem:

- Begin the costing process early – give people plenty of time to become familiar with ideas and procedures. The level of involvement can grow with their confidence.
- Involve people in the process of costing. This can be done at a number of levels. The greater sense of involvement people have in the creation of a budget then the more likely they are to stick to it in carrying out the service.

People with little or no experience of costing and budgeting may be operating under a double disadvantage of perceiving themselves as being "not good at figures". They may not attempt to interpret the figures for themselves because they don't expect to succeed in the task.

Consultation with staff or volunteers who actually deliver the service, and their immediate supervisors is essential. They are the people who have the detailed knowledge of the equipment, materials and time required to do the job; they understand the practical limitations of buildings, client ratios, staff rotas and so on. If you decide to go ahead with a contract their willing co-operation may well be an indispensable factor in securing the required quality of service; it will also make the financial management of the service much easier.

Active participation in costing is time consuming, but is worth it. The assumptions which form the basis for costing can be thrashed out in a group, and individuals or sub groups can be delegated to research particular items. An individual not familiar with figures can be paired with someone who is more confident as a "shadow". You must take care in putting together the figures to ensure that they really are all based on a shared set of assumptions. And some activities – like arithmetical checking – are better done outside of a meeting, by one or two individuals.

Circulate draft costings and other information in advance of meetings to give people a chance to digest information, and formulate alternatives and questions.

When people lack confidence they may seize on what they know. If they are not accustomed to handling large sums on paper you may find that the greatest amount of the committee's time and energy is expended on discussion of the least significant part of the budget. So meetings to discuss or approve costings also require prior thought, a structured agenda, and a briefing for the chair. When someone says "I know for a fact that you can get a widgets for £4.99 each so why should we pay £5.50?" you will need firm and sensitive chairing to (a) find out where and (b) get back to the agenda.

This tendency is not confined to the inexperienced. When I once presented a £55,000 grant application to a County Council Finance Committee the county treasurer, who managed millions, spent so long querying £50 in the budget for tea and coffee that there was no time for any other questions.

Don't try to chair a meeting in which you are also presenting costings.

A note on guessing

None of us knows for certain what will happen in the future.

Figure 1: PRESENTATION HELPS UNDERSTANDING

Take care over the presentation of costings on paper. Don't just present bald columns of figures. Attach some explanatory notes which highlight the priority points. These should concentrate the reader's attention on:

- the big sums of expenditure
- the consequences of commitments that may be entered into
- the certainty or otherwise of income
- the sequence and timetable of decisions to be taken by your organisation, purchasers/funders, and other parties
- any policy decisions required

How not to present figures

EXPENDITURES

Rent etc.	2,382.95
Stationery	400.00
Office	67.50
Salaries	11,961.45
Pay rise	456.66
Maintenance	£25
Miscellaneous	175.00
Insurance etc.	246.87
Auditor	350.00
Expenses	700.00
New Photocopier	895.25
VAT	289.97
Contingency	1,000.00
Total	18,950.65
Contract-extra costs	9,867.66
Grand total	**28,828.31**

Comments

- No date
- No information about the period or activity the figures refer to
- What is Miscellaneous?
- No reason to separate VAT out
- Kinds of expenditure (capital, revenue) mixed up
- What does "Contract extra costs" mean? extra to what?

Figure 1.2: THE SAME FIGURES RE-PRESENTED

The Pangloss Project Expenditure Budget 1992-3 (First draft – 31.11.92)

CORE ACTIVITIES		COMMENTS
Capital		
New photocopier	1,052	Cheaper than renewing lease on present machine
Revenue:		
Salary: Organiser–scale point 23	12,418	Inc. National Insurance & Pay award estimated at 7% from July
Organiser's expenses	700	Mainly travel & subsistance
Rent	2,383	Inc max possible service charge of £250
Telephone	76	
Stationery	470	Inc. new letterhead £200
Other office costs	203	Inc. Heating £110, Cleaning £68, Maintenance £25
Insurance	247	Employers' , Public Liability, Contents
Accountant & Audit	411	Based on last year's figure
Contingency	1,000	
Core activities: total revenue	17,909	
Total revenue and capital	18,960	

CONTRACT		
Capital		
Gardening tools	587	
Revenue		
Part-time worker – 0.6 scale point 19	8,693	Inc. National Insurance & Pay award estimated at 7%
Seeds and gardening materials	587	May be less (gifts in kind). Enough for 25 users.
Contract: Total Revenue	9,280	
Total revenue + capital	9,868	

SUMMARY	
CORE + CONTRACT COMBINED TOTAL CAPITAL	1,639
CORE + CONTRACT COMBINED TOTAL REVENUE	27,188
CORE + CONTRACT TOTAL CAPITAL + REVENUE	28,828

NB: All figures include VAT at 17.5% where applicable

> **Comments on Figure 1.2**
> - Core activities and contract separated
> - Capital and revenue separated
> - Totals summarised
> - Comments explain calculation
> - Labelled, numbered, dated.

Risk management

The more clearly you can specify what you want to cost then the easier the task will be. However, everyone involved in voluntary sector finance must learn to operate in an uncertain world. Organisations need to plan and implement services, without knowing for certain what resources will be available. Not only do you not know how much money you will have to spend, you also may not know when you are going to find out. You should be prepared for final agreement on contracts to be subject to the same sorts of delays that final agreements on grants used to be.

One of the few certainties is that there will be less than you would like to do the job. Hence the importance of costing to voluntary groups: if you don't know whether you are going to get £1,000 or £2,000 it is of great benefit to know what you can get for the money that you do eventually receive.

It also helps to view your costs not as a static picture like a snapshot but as a process happening in time, like a movie. Some things have to happen before other things can happen: premises must be converted before staff can be appointed; volunteer co-ordinators must be in post before volunteers can be recruited. And yet you still may not know what premises you are going to get, or how much they will cost to convert, or when staff and volunteers will be able to start taking on clients. With so much uncertainty you may feel tempted to throw up your hands in despair. Or seize the first available premises, or jump at a particular contract for the security of the income it offers.

In fact there are three elementary things that you can do to reduce the risks of uncertain situations.

The first is not to panic, and reach for short-term fixes; but to take a long-term view of the problem, and relate any possible solutions to your organisation's aims and objectives.

The second is to be organised and tidy; if you are surrounded by a chaotic world make sure that within your organisation there is some order, at least. Check that your decisions are clearly minuted; internal communications are clear and efficient; information is properly filed; and drafts of costings are clearly labelled, and so on.

Thirdly, you can make guesses about what is going to happen.

In preparing costings for activities to take place next year, or in three years' time, or which quite possibly do not even exist at present we must make predictions about what we think will happen. If we are lucky we can base calculations on figures from previous years, or from similar projects; in which case details such as numbers of staff and clients or users, rent for premises etc may be quite clear cut. All too often, however, we must guess.

Golden rules of guessing

1. Costs tend to rise while income tends to fall

   Unforeseen expenditure will always outweigh unforeseen savings

2. Things will take longer than you think

   Unforeseen delays will always outweigh unforeseen savings of time

Guessing is a natural human activity, which provided it is done sensibly can be very helpful in costing. Some simple precautions should be taken. The first is simple but easily overlooked: as soon as you have guessed – and before you guess again – make a note of the assumptions your guess is based on. The main source of error in guessing is not the guess itself but in guessing too often, and losing track of what each guess is based on.

Then you need to make your assessment of how accurate your guess is likely to be. For many of us the act of writing down figures seems to make them true; you must guard against this tendency by labelling your figures "rough estimate" or as appropriate. Giving a range is a useful device; you may not know exactly how much a computer will cost, but you do know won't get one for less than £850, and that you should be able to get what you need for no more than £2,000. Such minimum and maximum ranges can be added together to give minimum and maximum totals. For more on this technique see Chapter 11.

Lastly you must decide what – if anything – can be done to improve your guess, and anticipate when you will be able to turn your estimate into a firm figure. It may be very important to know that the true costs of an activity may not be known until after a contract is signed; for example where the level of demand for a given service fluctuates. You may under these circumstances wish to negotiate a particular method of pricing in your contract which will allow for this.

An overview of the costing process

This is a preliminary explanation, to give you a rough map of where you are going in using the following chapters of this book. We return to them in more detail in Part 4.

You need to think about costing a contract in three stages:

• Finding out what it would cost

• Setting a price

• Managing the contract.

At each stage you will hopefully be coming up with

increasingly detailed and accurate figures for the costs of providing a given service. But you will also be trying to answer different questions.

Deciding to seek a contract or not

This is a feasibility exercise, in which you are really trying to establish the conditions under which taking on a contract is viable and acceptable. You may not be able to pin down all the costs of the service in detail, though you will want to survey all the costs to be incurred. Your first aim will be to see if the actual costs of providing the specified service are within negotiating distance of the amount of money on offer. You will then be looking to be compare the effects on your organisation of going ahead with a contract with the effects of not going ahead.

You should be thinking strategically about the requirements of the contract in the context of other services you may wish to maintain and/or developments you may want to bring about. You need to look beyond the process of getting the contract and the first year's work. How do the consequences compare in 3 year or 5 or 10 years time?

Pricing a contract

Your first objective in this stage is to ensure that you have the most accurate possible estimate of all the costs you would incur in delivering the specified service. You may then need to devise appropriate Unit Costs to express them.

Your second objective is to understand how different methods of pricing the contract would affect your actual income and actual costs under varying circumstances.

Lastly you need to prepare for negotiation – the process of give and take.

You need to know what you can afford to give away on price, and what the cost would be of taking on more service.

Managing the contract

This is when the chickens come home to roost. You will need to collect information not just about whether expenditure is meeting predicted levels. You will also need a management system which monitors the level and quality of service, which provides adequate warnings of deviation from the plan; and which can decide on and implement corrective action effectively.

You may have to carry each kind of exercise several times as ideas about a proposed project develop, or as circumstances change. You will therefore be acquiring that most valuable asset – experience. You will make mistakes. As mistakes in costing can, almost by definition, be expensive, it is important that you learn from them. Rather than simply allowing your clients, volunteers and staff suffer you must ensure that it doesn't happen again. You should put the lessons you have learnt from financial management down in writing for the benefit of your colleagues and successors.

The need for a clear framework

As we have seen, costing is not a one-off exercise but a continuing process, that goes through several stages from preliminary feasibility, pricing and negotiation, to financial management and control. This offers us the chance to continuously revise and refine our predictions about the future as circumstances change, and as new information comes in. Because the content is in a continuous state of flux we need a clear structure or framework in which to deal with it.

Morag >> *a continuing story*

This book is necessarily comprehensive, covering the needs of the larger organisation as well as the smaller. In many cases these smaller groups need only apply the principles described in each chapter, without setting everything out in all the detail that may be essential for a contract worth hundreds of thousands of pounds. The story of Morag shows just such a small organisation tackling the same issues, but on a miniature scale.

Morag Stewart is the half-time paid co-ordinator, and only staff member, of the Munster Project. This ten year old charity arose out of a joint research project between the Department of Social Administration in Southtown Polytechnic, Loamshire Education Department, and Loamshire Social Services Southtown area office. The Project seeks to identify, through local primary schools, seven or eight year old children who are already at risk of educational and social failure as they grow up, and especially those for whom help within the family setting is unlikely to be successful – or is simply impractical. The children are instead introduced into 'clubs', where they have a chance to develop the social and personal skills and motivation so strikingly lacking in many such children. The clubs, once a week after school for a term, are run by pairs of trained volunteers recruited from trainee teachers, nurses and social workers at the Poly.

So successful was the project, initially intended as just a three year experiment, and so striking the later progress of the children at Secondary School compared to a matched control group, that all concerned in Southtown were determined to keep it going, A separate charity was formed, Morag's part-time salary was contributed by the Education Department, an office and the training of the volunteers by Social Services and the relatively modest running expenses of the clubs by a combination of local charities and the BBC Children in Need Appeal. At the start of this story Morag is organising 12 clubs a year (enthusiastically named by the children, and varying from the Crazy Gang to the Ghostbusters) for 140 children a year.

One day Morag needed to talk to Dr. Anderson, a local GP, about stories being told by a particular child. The doctor was interested to learn about the project as her large group practice, based at the New Southtown Health Centre and very recently endowed with responsibility for its own budgets, was interested in the mental health of local children; but the practice operated just outside the area covered by the Project). The following week she rang Morag; could she consider taking on a contract from the practice to run further clubs in their patch, perhaps six a year with ten children in each, for children about whom they were concerned? They thought that they might be able to justify a reasonable payment for this from the new incentives on offer from the Department of Health for preventive work of various kinds. Could Morag let her, Dr. Anderson, know the sort of costs that would be involved?

(Continued on Page 34.)

Chapter 2
A Framework for costing

This chapter explains how to understand your costs, by first breaking them down into headings or classes; then grouping them together into cost centres and lastly, if necessary, analysing how they may change with different levels of activity.

These are the basic building blocks out of which you can build a framework for financial planning and control.

"A place for everything and everything in its place"

Every item of expenditure and income whether planned (as in a budgeting exercise) or real (as in financial management) must have a home, a place where it belongs in a pre-determined framework. The framework you use needs to be appropriate to your organisation. It is the framework that enables you to record and subsequently retrieve useful financial information. The wrong framework will either lose useful data or give you irrelevant or misleading figures.

For example, managers in manufacturing industry want a financial system that enables them to take decisions such as whether to buy or make a particular component. They will need to bring together different pieces of information in order to compare an outside supplier's price with their own labour and materials costs, taking into account spreading overheads further and maximising investment in machinery.

The retail trade will have a different framework, as will local authorities. Large organisations require sophisticated and complex structures of financial planning and control.

Classes of expenditure and income

Cost centres

For most small and medium sized voluntary organisations a simpler framework is required. This book recommends one composed of two sets of categories – Classes of expenditure and income, and Cost Centres.

This scheme of classes and cost centres will provide you with a basis for

- Planning your finances – producing budgets and projections
- Recording your organisation's financial affairs – making entries in your book-keeping system
- Controlling your organisation's financial affairs by preparing reports from the books and comparing them with budgets.

Figure 2.1: COST CENTRES AND CLASSES

a Expenditure	b Cost Centre 1 Headquarters	Cost Centre 2 Day Centre Contract	Cost Centre 3 Outreach Contract	d Total
Total salary costs	24,521	13,821	14,567	**52,909**
Staff training	650	300	300	**1,250**
Rent	2,000	1,500	500	**4,000**
Heat & light	750	500	250	**1,500**
Office expenses	500	150	150	**800**
Telephone	1,100	250	350	**1,700**
Depreciation	350	400	200	**950**
Insurance	550			**550**
Legal	450	*g*		**450**
Audit	350			**350**
Travel			750	**750**
Volunteers expenses		2,750	2,750	**5,500**
Total expenditure c	**31,221**	**19,671**	**19,817** e	**70,709**

f Income				
Contracts		30,078	30,224	**60,302**
Contract management	20,814	(10,407)	(10,407)	**0**
Grants	6,000	*g*		**6,000**
Membership	4,407			**4,407**
Total income	**31,221**	**19,671**	**19,817**	**70,709**
Balance h (income - expenditure)	**0**	**0**	**0**	**0**

Classes

In the illustration above we have shown both classes of expenditure and of income. Because this is a book about *costing*, rather than about *funding* we will be concentrating here on classes of expenditure. However the remarks that follow about distinguishing and defining classes apply equally to income, though there will probably be a smaller number of them. Classes of Expenditure are sometimes called Heads of Expenditure, or Headings (when laid out in columns rather than rows).

You need to list all the kinds of expenditure that you may

incur in carrying out a contract. If that means your organisation is expanding or diversifying you may find that there are all sorts of new things you will need to spend money on. Part 3 of this book runs through the main kinds of expenditure most organisations are likely to incur. Looking at the classes used by other organisations can also give helpful pointers. It is worth spending a lot of time getting your classes of expenditure right.

Three key points in drawing up your list of classes of expenditure:

- Be *comprehensive*. Your classes need to cover all the expenditure you may incur (though a number of small headings can be combined in one class). If you start inventing new classes halfway through the year, you will play havoc with your book-keeping system, have to redraw budgets, and probably raise extra income.

- Keep it *as simple as possible* to operate. The more classes you have then the more time is consumed in financial planning, control and in book-keeping, and the more easily important issues are obscured by detail. Keep a sense of proportion, and use common sense in grouping things together.

- Make them *suit your purposes*. Beware of borrowing inappropriate models from other organisations. Pay particular attention to items of expenditure where you intend to recover the cost direct from the purchasing authority, or another funding body, such as the supply of appliances to clients.

It is in your interest to keep a clear written record of what each class includes and does not include, for your book-keeper, and anyone authorising expenditure to refer to.

Does your class "staff training" include travel to the training course? Do volunteers' travel expenses need to be separated from those of staff? Does the printing of the annual report come under "Publicity" or "Printing"? These are questions you must answer according to the circumstances of the organisation. The two most important points are that:

- you place all costs in one class or another;

- you use classes consistently.

It is helpful to group related classes together so that you may later consolidate them for producing summary reports, which show a total for each grouping, rather than the mass of individual class figures.

Figure 2.2: CONSOLIDATING CLASSES – salary costs	
Salary	11,961
National Insurance	1,250
Pension	598
Redundancy fund	12
Total salary costs	**13,821**

Contingency

You may see budgets with a class of expenditure called "Contingency" (sometimes called "Miscellaneous"). This can be very useful, but should be treated with care.

Using a Contingency class is a way of giving a margin for error and unforeseen circumstances. It is prudent to do this at the start of the costing process, when there are many uncertainties in the future. You may also wish to make use of it in longer-term forecasting, over 3 to 5 years. But by the time you have reached the stage of managing of a contract you should have reduced it to the absolute minimum.

The advantages of using a Contingency class

- it gives the organisation a measure of protection against

unforeseen circumstances, and allowance for changes in prices.

- if unused and retained it allows the organisation to build up reserves which offer more protection against larger scale disasters (loss of major funding, embezzlement by Executive Director, HQ riddled with dry rot) or which permit investment in new developments.

The disadvantages

- it can be used instead of thinking through exactly what will be needed; you could miss an area of expenditure, or a foreseeable rise in costs which could far outweigh a 5% or 10% contingency margin.
- if purchasers and funders see a blanket contingency they may reduce the contract price or grant accordingly. You may be able to get round this by distributing the contingency among other classes of expenditure. But you can't expect to add 5% or 10% to salary costs at specified grades, for example, without someone noticing.

For more suggestions on how to hide costs, see Chapter 12 *Pricing and Negotiation*. For more on finding useful bits of money see "Slush and Slippage" in Chapter 13 *Managing a Contract*.

A contingency allowance can give you some helpful flexibility. Voluntary organisations are meant to be very good at responding to new circumstances and being adaptable. This means you may have to spend money on something which you did not foresee. Don't use contingency to spare yourself the effort of working out what you will certainly need to spend money on.

Cost centres

A cost centre brings together all the classes of expenditure and classes of income that directly relate to a particular project, activity or service. Other items used for broadly the same concept are "profit centre" and "account".

Cost centres form a useful way of dividing up your organisation's finances so that different projects or departments can have their own budgets, share common "costs" and even "buy" services from each other. In Figure 2.1, for example the Contract Cost Centres (2) and (3) each "pay" Headquarters Cost Centre (1) £10,407 for the management of the contract. That is shown as income to Cost Centre (1) of £20,814, and in brackets as a "negative income" under Cost Centres (2) and (3).

You will need a separate cost centre at least for each and every contract you undertake. Larger and more complex services may need more than one cost centre per contract. You will also probably need one or more other cost centres for your activities and expenditure and income not directly related to contract work. Just as all the expenditure and income must go into one class or other, so must it all also be accounted for in one cost centre or another.

Purchasing authorities may want to inspect your accounts, to satisfy themselves that your costings are realistic and fair. But there may be financial details of other areas of activity – sponsorship deals for example – which you may well prefer not to disclose to those you are negotiating contracts with. Separate cost centres for contract work are particularly helpful if your organisation engages in campaigning activities. You may need to show that local authority funds you receive through contract or grant-aid are not being used to prepare "political publicity" or "promote homosexuality".

An example of using cost centres

The Flaxborough Trust runs a day centre for the elderly, employing two part-time staff on a grant from Social Services, and an unfunded evening youth club run by volunteers, both in the old Institute in the centre of town. Up until now all the costs and income have passed through one general account, as shown in Figure 2.3a

Figure 2.3a: FLAXBOROUGH TRUST COST CENTRES

Expenditure	
Total salary costs	10,000
Volunteers	500
Overheads	5,000
Total expenditure	**15,500**

Now however Flaxborough Council want to negotiate a contract for the day centre and a separate contract for a new outreach service, which will need extra staff.

The Flaxborough Trust therefore divide their accounts into three Cost centres:

Cost centre 01 – Contract 1 – Day Centre

Cost centre 02 – Contract 2 – Outreach

Cost centre 03 – General – All non-contract work

Figure 2.3b: FLAXBOROUGH TRUST COST CENTRES

Expenditure	Cost Centre 01 Contract 1 Day Centre	Cost Centre 02 Contract 2 Outreach	Cost Centre 03 General	Total
Total salary costs	10,000	5,000	0	15,000
Volunteers	0	0	500	500
Overheads	4,000	2,000	250	6,250
Total expenditure	**14,000**	**7,000**	**750**	**21,750**

Figure 2.3b shows how the Trust distributed the costs to the three cost centres.

The first row is Total Salary Costs and shows:

- The 2 part-time salaries at £10,000 under Cost Centre 1;
- The new half-time salary for the outreach service under Cost Centre 2; and
- No salaries being paid out of Cost Centre 3.

The second row is Volunteers and shows

- No expenditure for the 2 contract Cost Centres
- £500 for the youth club volunteers under Cost Centre 3.

When it came to looking at the Overheads in the third row the Trust recognised that the new outreach service will incur its own additional overheads. They also believed that the non-contract work incurs very little other expenditure, and in any case commands very little income. So they decided to distribute all the overheads amongst the cost centres according to a formula. They set £250 to Cost Centre 3, leaving the balance to be divided between the Cost centres 1 and 2 in the ratio of the numbers of staff working on each (2:1). Dividing costs is known as apportionment.

You may find it necessary to establish additional cost centres for services used in common by a number of Contract Cost Centres. The simplest example would be the photocopier. The photocopier Cost Centre pays out all charges for leasing and paper, and receives payments from other cost centres according to proportion of copies made by each.

You may wish to introduce other cost centres as your operations grow. You may find an office services cost centre, including phone, fax, photocopier, postage to be appropriate. Where several different services/contracts are based on a common building, you could use an Occupancy Cost Centre, which would pay out all charges for rent, rate, service charges, cleaning, depreciation and insurance of office equipment. It would receive payments from other cost centres using the building according to an agreed formula, based for example on the proportion of staff, floor area occupied, or hours of use. Other cost centres could be established for shared vehicles, or for a central management team (see Figures 5.1 and 5.2).

Figure 2.5: OCCUPANCY COST CENTRE

Expenditure

Rent	2000	
Rates	250	
Electricity	200	
Gas	350	
Water	100	
Cleaning	500	
Insurance	450	
Depreciation	300	
Total expenditure	**4150**	

Income

Cost centre X	2075	3 staff = 50% share
Cost centre Y	1369	2 staff = 33% share
Cost centre Z	705	1 staff = 17% share
Total income	**4150**	6 staff = 100% share

Don't overdo it

In practice you need to balance the usefulness of establishing new cost centres against the amount of work required to maintain the necessary financial records. There is an interdependence between cost centres, which can grow very rapidly. Changes to costings in one cost centre will have consequences for others. Clearly, in order to get a picture of your organisation's overall financial position, it is necessary to bring all the cost centres together, and show them on a single piece of paper or on a single computer spreadsheet.

The more cost centres and classes you use then the more

detailed information you will get about your operations. However be warned that such detail can swamp broad trends. It can also swamp your book-keeper. Any organisation which anticipates using more than 3 or 4 cost centres should seriously investigate a simple computerised accounting package (see Appendix 2 *Using Computers*).

Categorising costs by function

Having got our framework for pigeonholing costs by class and by cost centre, we also need a way of understanding how costs behave under different circumstances. To do this we can divide them into categories defined by their function, the frequency with which they occur and by their relationship to different levels of service provided.

There are many different approaches to categorising costs, depending on the purpose of the costing exercise and the nature of the activity. The costing categories and procedures used in manufacturing or in the retail trade for example differ from each other, and from those used in the public sector. The terminology may differ; or more confusingly the same words can be used with different meanings. In negotiating contracts you should be quite sure that both purchaser and provider mean the same things when they use a particular phrase. Terms such as "on costs", "running costs" and "overheads" should be treated with caution. There may be much that the public sector can learn from the private sector. However the wholesale introduction of technical terms as buzz-words and their inappropriate application to activities in another sector is not very helpful.

Most voluntary organisations entering into contracts will make use of the following kinds of costs:

- **Capital** – one off purchase of major assets – buildings, vehicles and equipment. Besides this direct one-off cost, there is also usually a further annual 'depreciation' charge; this is money that has to be set aside each year to replace

31

the capital equipment, say a minibus, in due course. See Chapter 4.

All other spending is **revenue**. There are four kinds of revenue costs:

- **Set-up costs** – one-off spending on goods or services necessary to start the operation. The practical distinction between capital expenditure and revenue set-up costs is firstly one of size; minor items like lamps or staplers are not usually counted as capital. The second more critical test is whether or not you intend to depreciate the item (set money aside each year to fund a replacement when it is worn out). Revenue items cannot be depreciated.

- **Fixed direct costs** – direct means that these are directly and wholly incurred by carrying out an activity. Under this heading you would include all the salaries of staff delivering the service to clients, their working clothes, their training, the cost of leaflets they use etc. Where the cost remains the same regardless of the level of activity these are known as Fixed direct costs. You must still insure and pay road tax for a mini-bus whether it does 5 miles a week or 500.

- **Variable direct costs** refers to those direct costs which fluctuate according to the amount of activity undertaken: the cost of petrol, oil and servicing the minibus will vary according to the amount of use it gets. Other examples might be other kinds of consumables – stocks of food for user's meals, craft materials; or they may even include casual or sessional staff or volunteers' expenses.

- **Indirect costs** – These are costs which are indirectly incurred by an activity, and are usually shared by several activities. They include a due proportion of the costs of administration and management, and any other support activities an organisation undertakes in order to be able to provide the service, including the cost of negotiating the contract itself. They are generally fixed.

The nature of the service, and the duration of the contract will influence your classification of some costs as Fixed or Variable; the distinction between Direct and Indirect costs can also be blurred. Where there are ambiguities, which you choose matters less than using it consistently.

Fixed costs will not remain fixed if there is a substantial change in the volume of an activity. In costing a service employing one advice worker you would normally regard the salary as a fixed cost. If you change the specification of the activity so as to require two advice workers you should still regard the salary costs as fixed. If you have had to re-calibrate your fixed direct costs in this way then your indirect costs – hitherto apparently also fixed – may well need adjustment too.

How variable costs vary in relation to the volume of the service may change at very high or very low volumes of service. These points are explored in more detail in Chapter 12.

CLASSES AND CATEGORIES OF COSTS

Some classes of expenditure will occur under more than one kind of cost. You may find it helpful later (when drawing up budgets and working out Unit Costs) if you have calculated these separately. Take Salaries, for example:

Set-Up Costs
A team leader spends two months doing initial research into users' needs and the delivery of the service.

Fixed direct costs
You take on a team of 4 staff who will do most of the work of providing the service.

Variable Costs
If demand for the service rises above a certain point you will take on temporary or sessional staff.

Indirect Costs
The contract also takes up 50% of the time of a Project Manager, 25% of the time of both the Finance Officer and the Chief Administrator, and 10% of the General Secretary.

Morag >> *a continuing story* (*from Page 19*)

Morag knew her Management Committee were only too keen to see the project spread more widely, but before discussing Dr Anderson's suggestion with them she wanted to have a clear idea of the costs involved. At present she just kept a cashbook record of her receipts of about £3,000 a year from the various charities supporting her, and of the payments made. These she recorded under six headings (or classes):

Staff expenses (eg. her own car allowance)
Printing and publicity
Volunteer's travel expenses and "thank you" parties,
Club venue hire and costs
Children's travel (by Loamshire Community Transport)
Club running expenses (food, games, materials etc.)

As a start she wrote down this list on a sheet of paper, adding Salary and Premises/office costs as further classes or headings (though she had no record of these, other than her own payslips, as they were provided for her). She then added a second column (or Cost Centre) on the right of the page to which she could add figures for the proposed expansion.

Munster Project – Costs

	Main Project	New Project
Salary	£7,050?	£?
Premises/office costs	£?	£?
Staff expenses	£450	£?
Printing and publicity	£375	£?
Volunteer's travel/expenses	£480	£?
Club venue hire/costs (usually donated)	£200	£?
Children's travel	£500	£?
Club running costs	£1,200	£?

(Continued on Page 50)

WHAT TO COST AND HOW

This part of the book aims to help you to identify all the costs you will incur in providing a service under contract, and arrive at accurate and realistic figures for these. Costings date very quickly. The figures that are quoted here are for illustration only, and should not be taken as a guide to the actual sums you will need to pay.

You should also think very carefully about the service you would provide to ensure that you include any other costs which are not listed here.

Read this section and as you go through mark points you will need to return to when you are carry out your costings. Don't forget you don't need or want to have a different class or heading for every cost; but every cost you will incur *must* appear in one class or another.

Chapter 3
Staff and Volunteers

Costing Paid Staff

Your starting point in making your calculations should be the service specification. If this has not yet been drawn up or agreed, write your own for what you propose to do. From this you should be able to determine how many staff will be required, and at what grades of pay. For most voluntary organisations the major element in the cost of a contract will be staff, so it's worth making sure that your estimates are as realistic and accurate as possible.

Bear in mind that the specification may spell out in some detail the tasks required to actually deliver the service, but omit associated activities like travel to and from clients and so on. If actual staff numbers are specified then you should check carefully that they are realistic both for your organisation and the actual service you are to carry out.

Comprehensive, well thought-through job descriptions are a great aid in determining not just scales of pay but also the number of staff required to provide a given level of service.

Jobs in the voluntary sector often require combinations of skills and experience, and a degree of responsibility and flexibility, which are not recognised by pay structures designed for hierarchical bureaucracies. It is worth investigating what other voluntary organisations pay comparable staff. Adapting a recognised scheme is probably

CALCULATING STAFF TIME AVAILABLE FOR DELIVERY OF SERVICE

One full-time member of staff obviously cannot provide a service for 7 days a week, 52 weeks a year. So just how much time can they spend on the tasks set out in the specification?

1 Full Time Equivalent person year after 24 days annual leave and 8 public holidays

= 228 working days = 46 x 5-day working weeks.

Less say 7 days of training per year (4 days "in-house" and 1 three-day external course)

= 221 working days = 44.2 x 5-day working weeks

In each 5 day/35 hour week each member of staff will also have to

Attend Staff Meetings, Supervision sessions – 2 hours

Preparation of reports, other administration – 2.5 hours

Travel to Clients – 5 hours

Liaison with other agencies 2.5 hours

Total deductions of 12 hours from 35 hour working week

= 22 hours per working week

Maximum possible time available for actual client contact per year

= 44.2 weeks x 22 hours = 972.4 hours

That example is based on one full-time member of staff. What if you employ two half-time staff? Depending on how the work is to be divided you may find that you must increase the time allocated to training, supervision, and attendance at staff meetings.

more sensible than devising your own. But make sure that you do use a system; a sequence of ad-hoc agreements with individual staff or projects can lead to disaster.

Having said that, your organisation must in the end make a judgement of what you need to pay to secure the staff you need. The decision will be greatly helped by a good, detailed job description, which spells out the aim of the job, the tasks (in priority order), to whom responsible, the responsibilities (staff, cash, clients) and which is supported by a person specification clearly distinguishing essential and desirable qualities.

Grades and rates of pay

Most voluntary organisations want to offer their staff terms and conditions that are tied to national agreements used in relevant parts of the public sector, where pay awards are negotiated annually.

One of the most commonly used are the National Joint Committee (NJC) scales designed for Administrative, Professional, Technical and Clerical posts in local authorities. NJC gives rates of pay for posts ranging from clerical and executive (scales 1-6) through to Senior Officers (SO 1 & 2) to a number of Principal Officers (PO) grades.

Within each there are 3 or 4 points, often called scale points or spinal points, or abbreviated to "scp". Figure 3.1 gives NJC scales for 1991-2.

The NJC publishes an annual "Purple Book" which gives full details of ancillary terms and conditions such as travel and subsistence allowances. It also provides a skeleton structure distinguishing levels of responsibility, but stopping short of actually grading jobs. That remains the privilege of individual employers.

Employers generally want to appoint at the bottom of the scale, at the lowest point; staff then progress up to the top of the scale by annual increments, a spinal point at a time. (But some employees may be able to negotiate a higher starting point because of qualifications, not taking a drop in earning from previous employment etc). Some organisations also operate banding arrangements which, under certain circumstances, allow staff to move on to the next scale, rather than get stuck at the top point in a scale.

Figure 3.1: NJC SCALES 1991-2

SCP	Salary from 1.7.91	Scale	SCP	Salary from 1.7.91	Scale
1	5,007		29	15,066	
2	5,346		30	15,570	SO1
3	5,778		31	16,068	
4	6,129		32	16,545	SO2
5	6,561	Scale 1	33	17,040	
6	6,963		34	17,529	
7	7,359		35	17,898	POA
8	7,830		36	18,375	
9	8,340		37	18,900	
10/11	8,901	Scale 1/2	38	19,461	
12	9,093	Scale 2	39	20,097	
13	9,336		40	20,637	
14	9,516		41	21,186	PO Scales
15	9,723	Scale 3	42	21,726	
16	9,963		43	22,278	
17	10,215		44	22,821	
18	10,422		45	23,340	
19	10,824	Scale 4	46	23,910	
20	11,232		47	24,459	
21	11,652		48	25,002	
22	11,961		49	25,539	
23	12,318	Scale 5			
24	12,726				
25	13,134				
26	13,563				
27	14,019	Scale 6			
28	14,484				

Calculating salaries

The facts you need to gather may include:

- For new staff: recruitment cost, numbers, full or part time, start date, grade on appointment, length of contract (if fixed term), increments due in this and future years, current rates for grades, actual or likely pay annual award and date it takes effect, rate of National Insurance and Pension contributions (if any);

- Existing staff: numbers, full or part time, grade now, length of contract (if fixed term), increments due in this and future years, current rates for grades, actual or likely annual award and date it takes effect, rate of National Insurance and Pension contributions (if any);

- Staff transferred from another employer: what obligations do you inherit in terms of grades of pay, increments, terms and conditions of employment, employer's contribution to pension scheme etc?

Pay awards

Most organisations budget on a financial year running from April to March. However national pay agreements often start later in the year. So you may need to predict what the level of pay award will be and make an adjusted calculation for the whole year. NJC pay awards generally take effect from July 1st.

Annual increments can add an additional layer of calculation, depending on when staff receive them. If the policy in your organisation is to award increments on a set date – 1st April, for example, then it is relatively simple. Some organisations, however, pay increments on the anniversary of joining the organisation.

Making a prediction about the level of settlement is much easier if you know:

- how big a claim the union side has put in, and

- how small a counter offer the employer's side have made.

You will also want to take into account the rate of inflation, trends in other wage settlements, central government action to restrain public expenditure or curb wages, the proximity of a general election etc.

Though you will be looking to pick a certain percentage increase, remember that some pay settlements are weighted towards lower-paid staff. A headline increase of 6% may mask an increase of 7% for lower grades and 5% for higher grades. The consequences for your organisation will depend on the balance in your organisation. As well as pay, other terms and conditions of employment are usually renegotiated annually. Car user allowances are generally revised at the same rate as the main settlement, for example. There has been a trend in recent years towards bargaining across the whole "remuneration package" – trading lower pay rises for

---

CALCULATING PAY AWARDS

THE CASE OF ELIZABETH BUNTY (a fictional example)
Elizabeth was on Scale point 27 at 31st March 1991
£14,019

Her annual increment is due on 1st April 1991 so she moves up to Scale point 28

Scale point 28 at 1st April 1991 was £14484

We assume a pay award of 6% at 1st July 1991, so £14,484 + 6% = £15,353

So Elizabeth's gross salary for the Year April 1991 to March 1992 is made up as follows

April to June: 3 months at £14,484 per annum = £3,621

July to March: 9 months at £15,353 per annum =£11,515

So Elizabeth's gross salary for the year will be = £15,136

This last figure is the one you will use to calculate Employers' National Insurance Contributions etc.

---

longer holidays, or maternity/paternity leave. Such changes in your staff's terms and conditions may incur costs for your organisation.

Note that in all pay negotiations between unions and employers there can be delays in reaching agreement. In the case of NJC the uncertainty has gone on into September, so that staff do not receive the increase until the October pay packet, when they receive three months' backdated pay at the new rate. This state of affairs may have consequences for your cash flow.

National Insurance

Employers must pay a contribution to the National Insurance scheme, in addition to the Employee's contribution. At the time of writing this is done at 10.45% of Employee's gross salary, or 9% for those working less than 21 hours per week. Other rates apply for people on very low incomes. For details on liability for National Insurance and current rates check with the Department of Social Security.

Pension

Employers may contribute to a pensions scheme for their employees, though not necessarily for temporary or part-time staff. The rate is normally a percentage (5% approximately) of gross salary – the pension fund managers will supply details.

Employers' liability insurance

You are required by law to insure against employees' claims for injury or illness. See under Insurance in Chapter 5.

Some less obvious costs of employing people

You must also consider how you will meet your contractual obligations to provide a service if and when your staff are not at work. You will obviously need to arrange sufficient staff to cover for each other's annual leave, for Public Holidays (if necessary) and subsequent time off in lieu; and for time spent in training. Does the contract specification allow the service to close during staff holidays?

You must also anticipate unpredictable but inevitable contingencies such as sickness, resignations, dismissals and suspensions, jury service, long-term illness, maternity/paternity leave and compassionate leave.

How will you cope with such a contingency? How will you meet your contractual obligations? Your options include asking part-time staff to work full time, secondments from other departments or organisations, recruiting new staff and or using an agency. When you know how you would provide the necessary cover you can calculate a cost.

Staff (or sub-contractors) on short term contracts, and staff available at short notice usually command a higher wage or fee. Urgent recruitment is likely to be more costly, as is a crash course of training for new staff.

It is particularly difficult for small organisations to provide for such contingencies – fewer staff and smaller budgets generally mean less flexibility. But because the consequences for meeting the demands of providing a service can be so grave you should make some allowance.

It is also prudent to make some provision for the regrettable contingency of having to make redundancy payments. The statutory minimum for a 35 year old, for example, is one week's wage for every year of service over two years. This can be financed by a levy on salaries which is set aside into a separate fund. The rate of the levy could be 1% or 2% or 5%, and will depend on the risk; it should be higher in smaller organisations. Alternatively, you may wish to negotiate redundancy protection clauses into the contract.

Recruitment costs

These are often forgotten, but can be substantial. Advertising rates in local or national newspapers vary enormously, and are often negotiable. Ring the paper's Advertising Sales Department and ask for a quote. Ask them to explain the pricing system. Display and semi-display adverts are usually priced per column/centimetre of space. Ask for discounts. Check whether the price includes VAT and typesetting, if you are not supplying camera-ready artwork.

And what will the following cost you?

- Preparing art-work for advertisement,
- Preparing, printing and distributing a flyer for mailings etc,
- Preparing and copying job descriptions, application forms, equal opportunities monitoring forms,
- Postage – sending out forms (ask for stamped addressed envelopes?),
- Time spent answering the phone and processing applications,
- Interviews – venue, candidates' expenses.

Recruiting or replacing staff always takes more time than you think, so give generous margins to your start date.

Self-employed contractors

Should you be employing staff for the purpose? For some specialist kinds of work a self-employed contractor or consultant might be more appropriate. They operate in an open market, and in theory can charge what they can get. However it is advisable to peg your offer of fee to some sort of scale e.g. an NJC grade plus 15% to cover National Insurance and Pension Contributions plus a premium for a short term contract or a retainer to guarantee availability. You will need to check that your contractors are genuinely self-employed (see Inland Revenue Leaflet) or you may be liable for their Income Tax. You should also check that your contract with the purchaser permits you to sub-contract; and that your contract with the sub-contractor gives you the power to ensure you meet the purchaser's requirements.

Supervision

As well as looking at how much work you are asking your service delivery staff to do you should also assess the workload on supervisors and first line managers if your organisation is large enough to have such people. What ratios are practical? A contract that brings an expansion in your services will almost certainly mean that some of your key service delivery staff will be needed to move up to supervise new workers. They may need training to carry out supervision effectively.

Costing volunteers

Volunteers are essential to the provision of services in many, if not most voluntary organisations. Yet there are many anxieties about the effects of contracts on volunteers and their relationships with users, paid staff, volunteer using organisations, and each other. This section aims to help you clarify the consequences for your organisation.

Your first task is to define the various tasks and roles that volunteers would undertake in providing the service.

You need to consult the draft contract (if available), the contract specification, and any accompanying quality statements to see if any of these contain any requirements or standards for the use of volunteers. (If they do not it may be in your interest to draft some and negotiate them in.)

The NCVO's Basic Principles for the Voluntary sector calls on organisations to "use volunteers and charitable funds to improve the quality of service rather than substitute for paid labour or under-cut competing bids."

You will face pressure to cut costs and shift tasks from paid staff to unpaid volunteers, both in the delivery of the service itself, and in the support echelons. You may also face pressure to put paid staff in to carry out more quickly and efficiently some tasks which have in the past been done by volunteers. You need to examine what impact such steps would have on the quality of the service you are aiming to provide, and on the non-contractual elements of your organisation's work.

Having identified and defined the appropriate kinds of tasks for volunteers, you must then make an appraisal of the level of service your volunteers can provide and that you can support. At this point you will probably wish to consult with volunteers and volunteer organisers on your staff about realistic targets for your volunteers' work.

How many volunteers? What is their pattern of work? Ten volunteers each putting in two hours a week may create a different pattern of costs from two volunteers each putting in ten hours a week. Just as with paid staff you need to allow a margin for "non-productive" work – not actually delivering the service but attending meetings, receiving training, and supervision, carrying out monitoring tasks etc. But because they are volunteers these elements are often harder to prescribe.

With a clear picture of the numbers and distribution of volunteers required, and the tasks they will carry out you should be in a position to cost the following items:

• **Recruitment**
  In addition to staff (volunteer organiser) time, there may be payments for the design, printing and distribution of leaflets, posters etc; paid-for advertising (and/or staff time to organise sponsored ads and editorial coverage).

Are you looking for certain kinds of volunteers – with particular skills or experience, or from particular communities? Do you need to recruit them to a deadline? If so what extra costs will achieving that incur – in payments or staff time?

You should also consider the impact of recruiting volunteers for the contract service on the supply or availability of volunteers for other areas of your organisation's work.

- Selection

  What process will you use? Who will be involved, and for how much time? What about the administrative tasks of, for example, carrying out police checks and other screening?

- Training

  Do volunteers need any training or induction before they start? What about training subsequently? Who will carry out the training? Who will cover for the volunteers while they are being trained? If training is external what are the course fees, and travel and subsistence expenses? If internal who will organise, prepare and lead the training sessions? Where will you do it, and what training materials and aids will be needed?

- Supervision

  Who will supervise the volunteers, and how much time will that take them? Do you need to have a supervisor permanently on call? What about the implementation of your quality assurance system and monitoring procedures?

  What are the costs of implementing your Equal Opportunities policy in relation to volunteers, and extending your Health & Safety cover?

- Insurance

  See Chapter 5.

- **Expenses**

  What payments will you need to make to volunteers to cover their expenses for travel, meals, board and lodging, laundry, telephone calls, expenditure incurred on clients' behalf?

  Or will you be providing some of these in kind? What cost centre will bear that cost?

  Do you need to provide any materials, special clothing or equipment for volunteers' use?

  Will you be making any other payments – honoraria or allowances – to volunteers? Are these subject to national insurance contributions and/or tax?

  Who will carry out the financial administration (including cost control) for volunteers, and how much time will it take them?

  Are the "terms and conditions" you are introducing for contract volunteers the same as those for non-contract volunteers? Will these have to be harmonised, and if so at what cost to the rest of the organisation?

- **Training Others**

  Do you need to provide training in working with volunteers for:

  > your supervisors, your managers & members of management committees
  >
  > other staff
  >
  > care managers

Estimating travel cost of staff and volunteers

Travel undertaken by staff in order to provide a contract service may be calculated from a daily, weekly or monthly estimate of journeys needed.

If public transport is to be used, remember to allow for fare increases during the life of the budget, and for any savings which may be made through season tickets, saver strips etc.

If staff use their own cars they will be entitled to claim travel expenses under their terms and conditions of employment. NJC agreements provide for either Casual or Essential Car User rates. Payment to the Casual Car User is based on rates which taper down in 4 stages as the mileage increases. By contrast the Essential Car User is entitled to 2 lower mileage rates and a fixed annual lump sum payment.

Remember that such travel allowances may well be revised upward in annual pay agreements.

If volunteers use their own cars you must have a clear policy and system for reimbursing them – commonly the same arrangement as staff. Note that volunteer drivers claiming mileage expenses in excess of 5000 miles a year may be liable to tax on their expenses. NCVO or your local CVS may be able to advise on alternative arrangements, but it could cost your organisation more to fully reimburse these volunteer drivers. See the next chapter for costing the organisation's own vehicles.

It may simplify financial control to count travel for other purposes against the relevant class of expenditure. For example travel to and from training courses may be charged to Training rather than Travel. Make sure that your book-keeper (and staff making claims) are aware of the policy you decide upon.

Morag >> *a continuing story* (from Page 34)

Morag reckoned (and her management committee agreed with her, on the rare occasions it got around to meeting) that her time was already fully stretched just meeting her present obligations. Nor, as she had small children to look after, could she consider working longer hours. However, could this new idea, of a further set of Munster Clubs for the new Southtown Health Centre, be the means of justifying her long term dream –

of a part-time assistant who would take on the routine administrative load and free her to concentrate on working with the clubs and the volunteers.

She decided to base her costings on this assumption, and started to work out the extra money needed for such a person, and put this tentatively in the right hand column:

Munster Project – Costs

	Main Project	New Project
Salary	£7050?	£4,000?

However, a short chat with the Admin Officer in the Social Services area office where she worked made two things clear. First, there was no reason why the main project should bear all her costs and the new development all those of her assistant – after all, they would each be working some of the time for each. Secondly, her own salary costs were considerably more than those shown on her pay slips – she had ignored National Insurance and Employers Pension Contributions, and the cost of her assistant would need to be adjusted likewise. She decided to split their combined costs 2/3 to the main project (running 12 clubs) and 1/3 to the new proposal (with six clubs). She knew that setting up the new clubs would be harder work than repeating the existing ones, but they would also be more fun! She also added a flat 10% to the figures on the assumption that the new project could not start until the next year, and this would accommodate the intervening inflation.

	Main Project	New Project
Salary (P/T Co-ordinator and P/T Assistant)	£9,000	£4,500

(Continued on Page 73)

Chapter 4

Premises, Equipment and Other Assets

Capital spending

Care managers with whom you have to negotiate may see capital expenditure as falling outside the scope of service contracts. Nevertheless your organisation may need to embark on capital expenditure in order to provide a service to the required quality standard. A common example will be making premises fully accessible to people with disabilities, or children in prams and push chairs.

Whether the funding for capital expenditure comes through the contract, or through "soft" loans, direct grant aid and/ or other fund-raising efforts it will have an effect on the cost of providing a service. If you are costing a capital programme you should seek advice from your accountant, your local authority and any other voluntary organisations with relevant experiences. The advice of a surveyor and architect should also be sought for costing any building or conversion work.

Capital expenditure is about investing in the long-term future of your organisation and its work. As in any costing exercise you need to begin with a specification, to which you can then put a price, or range of prices. In drawing up your specification you must plan for future needs as well as the demands of getting this year's contract going. It really does pay to spend time getting capital spending right first time. If you get it wrong you will never recover the full value of an item by selling it – if you are able to sell it. You will certainly never recover the cost of the work of costing and purchasing a second time.

It can take a long time to complete a capital purchase programme. The actual purchase can be protracted. There can be delivery delays. To get premises fitted out or equipment installed and working can be a very time consuming business.

Delays on the capital programme can have effects on revenue. You may need to take on expensive short-term leases of premises or equipment in order to provide a service. Key staff may be diverted from service provision to the 1001 jobs there are to be done to chase up and complete the purchase or conversion of premises. Or you may not be able to provide a service at all, or only start at a lower volume. That in turn may reduce your income, adversely affect your cash flow, and so increase your interest payments.

You should take legal advice before entering into a large-scale purchase contract, not least to ensure that you include appropriate penalty clauses for delays.

Premises

Buy v. lease? – a summary of the arguments

Purchase of existing property

Advantages: long term security, lower revenue costs, may make use of capital grant aid (if available), or once-off fund-raising effort, can convert to needs, and sub-let to create revenue income.

Disadvantages: problem of availability, delay, more

conversion work/time/money required; long-term maintenance commitment

Purchase new build/part of development:

Advantages: custom built, could be private sector "donation"

Disadvantages: very expensive, long lead time.

Commercial Lease

Advantages: more available, in more suitable locations, more quickly

Disadvantages: higher revenue costs, subject to upward rent reviews, major conversion to needs may be impossible or uneconomic.

Other options include

- Sharing or subletting other organisation's unused space
- Use of purchasing authority premises (see Chapter 12 Pricing and Negotiation)
- Local authorities may also offer long leases in development areas at a high initial premium, nearly as much as freehold purchase, but with fixed peppercorn rents.

Using existing premises

If you already occupy the premises you would be using in order to provide a contract service then you should not have too much difficulty in arriving at an accurate estimate of your costs.

Bear in mind that if you use the premises for other purposes you may not be able to charge the whole cost of running the premises to the contract cost centre. It may be necessary to create a "premises" cost centre to which the contract and other cost centres contribute in proportion to the use they make of it. You could calculate this on the basis of floor area, or numbers of staff, or hours of use that each cost centre makes of the building.

You should think carefully about the requirements of the contract in relation to the capacity of your building, and the impact providing the service would have on other uses.

The Prszewalski Association has a large meeting room which is used once a month for training events for the whole organisation, and by other groups paying hire charges which total £300 a year. In order to take on a contract from Middlemarch Health Authority the Association needs to use the room every day. So in apportioning the costs of the premises the Association could weight the contribution made by the contract cost centre by adding two increments to cover:

- The additional expense incurred by the Association of hiring another venue for its monthly training events;
- The loss of £300 income (with due allowance made for inflation in future years)

Taking over premises

If the contract you are costing is taking over a service on the premises of the purchasing authority (because it has hitherto been provided in-house) you will need to examine the draft contract and specification carefully to see what arrangements are proposed for your occupation of the premises, and what liability your organisation will have for the running costs of the premises.

You will then want to look carefully at the costs of running the premises. Do not take any financial information supplied by the purchasing authority at face value.

Their figures for a given establishment may not reflect the actual costs incurred at that site, because:

- The accounting system was not set up to record that level of detail;
- Accounting conventions used by local authorities may mean some expenditure incurred in running premises

has not been counted because it has been set against the budget of another department, or met from central funds.

- Errors may be made in the complex task of reconstructing financial information

The electricity board may have billed Middlemarch Council for all of its 10 day centres and 10 residential establishments on one invoice. So the figures for electricity costs for the Casaubon Day Centre may have nothing to do with the number of units consumed there because they have been calculated as a proportion of the costs of all the centres, say 1/20th. Over the years quite complex and varying formulae of apportionment have grown up in purchasing authority departments, and some of them will have diverged a long way from the reality. However if you are taking over the account for the electricity supply to the Casaubon Day Centre you will have to pay bills to the electricity supply company for actual units used there.

Maintenance and repair costs should also be examined carefully. If your contract stipulates that they are your responsibility then go and see what sort of state the premises are in. If the maintenance and repair costs for recent years quoted by the purchasing authority are low then work may be desperately needed; if they are high it may be because there are a lot of unresolved problems.

In taking over an in-house contract the important costing question is what it will cost you to provide the service, not what the purchasing authority says it used to cost them.

In using past figures for predicting the costs of premises remember to make due allowance for any change in the nature or volume of use that the contract will require.

If your building has only been used during the day, and your contract means that you will now be using it four evenings a week as well, then you will plainly have to make an allowance for additional heating, lighting and possibly cleaning.

You should look closely at the contract, the specification, and any quality statements to ensure that the premises can actually be used to deliver required service.

Are they big enough, in the right place, and accessible? (see **Access** section in Chapter 7). Is it warm, dry and well-lit? Are there enough toilets? Is it secure? Is it the right kind of environment for the service?

In a Yorkshire mill town an imposing 19th century building was beautifully refurbished as an education and activity centre for elderly people. But they would not come in. When they were growing up, the place was the work-house.

What will you have to spend in order to bring the premises up to scratch?

You will want to ensure that any premises used meet all the relevant regulations relating to Fire, Health and Safety and Environmental Health, Building and Planning controls, as well as the relevant sections of **Factories Act** and the **Office Shops and Railway Premises Act**.

The local authority will also have a range of standards which residential establishments will have to comply with.

Fire: the fire brigade will inspect your premises and advise you of the measures to be taken in respect of alarms, signing, exits and fire-fighting equipment. Similarly the police Crime Prevention Officer should be called in to advise on security arrangements (see also **Insurance** in Chapter 5).

Leased premises

When taking on leased premises it is customary for the lessee (you) to met the legal costs of the lessor (the landlord) as well as your own. The lessor's solicitor will draw up the lease; your solicitor (and you) should look at it and make any counter-proposals, and how much you will have to pay in legal costs will depend on how much time the solicitors spend arguing about it.

Most leases that run for more than 3 or 5 years stipulate rent reviews. If there has been a considerable rise in office rents during a lease, or between reviews you should budget for a large increase at lease renewal or at rent review time.

In addition to the rent most leases commit you to paying a quarterly service charge. This is usually calculated by taking the cost of cleaning and maintaining common areas of a building and services (lift, stairs lighting, possibly heating) and dividing it between the tenants in the proportion of the floor area occupied. So the landlord or agent may not be willing to give a firm figure until he knows what those bills have come to. Ask for last year's figure, or their estimate of this year's.

In managed premises service charges will be a lot higher, and may be rolled into a total weekly or monthly "rental charge"; in either case the lease or the rental agreement should specify what the service charge covers.

Rates and rate relief

Business rates are worked out on the basis of a uniform rate in the pound, set by the government. So you need to know both the rateable value of the property, and the level at which the rate (sometimes called the multiplier) is set. Thus for premises with a rateable value of £2,000 and a rate of 34.8p in the pound the full rate bill will be £696 (£2,000 x 0.348).

However if the property is used "wholly or mainly for charitable purposes" by an organisation or institution "established for charitable purposes" then you can claim mandatory relief of 80% – in the above example reducing the bill to £139.20. In addition local authorities have quite wide discretionary powers to grant 100% relief to non profit-making bodies.

In making forecasts for future years bear in mind that revaluation of the property may lead to a sharp increase in rate bills. A revaluation is more likely to take place when a new lease is assigned, or if a property is subdivided or rehabilitated.

If you are running any kind of residential establishment then you should take advice on any liability you – or your staff or volunteers – may have for poll tax or the new council tax payments.

You should keep abreast of new legislation on the whole system of local authority finance. Change is inevitable, despite the government staying unchanged after the 1992 General Election. New rules on reliefs, or a reduction in domestic contributions, and/or government support could push the uniform business rate up.

Heating

If you are taking over premises, ask previous tenants about heating costs – last years bills (with a due allowance for fuel price rises) may give a good indication of heating costs. Remember that you may be making different use of the premises.

You may also need to buy or lease heaters.

Make allowance for maintenance of the heating system, possibly through a flat rate contract.

If you will be occupying the premises for more than 6 months is it worth spending money now on insulation and energy conservation?

Lighting

Assess bills as for heating. Many commercially leased premises have fluorescent strip lighting which may not be appropriate for your use. Do you also need to provide desk or working lamps? Do your staff, volunteers or users have any special lighting needs – to avoid glare on VDU screens, for example? What about evening use of the premises?

Ventilation

Is this adequate for the use you will be making of the building?

Water and sewage

Assuming you are not engaged in a manufacturing process which needs lots of water and produces lots of effluent, then non-domestic users pay the water company in one of two ways:

- Charges for water and for sewage are levied as a rate in the pound on the rateable value of your premises; these may be increased annually.

- Water companies prefer you to use a water meter. You pay for so much per unit of water supplied plus a supply standing charge, plus so much per unit of sewage plus a sewage standing charge. Sewage is calculated as a fixed percentage of the water consumed – usually about 95%.

Group homes will probably qualify for domestic tariffs, especially if there is no social worker or carer sleeping in. Domestic standing charges are (at present) lower than non-domestic. Relatively few domestic premises are metered. But the rateable value method will be phased out by the year 2,000, though at present it is not clear what system will be used to replace it for domestic consumers. Metering could dramatically increase the water costs of large households in low rateable value premises. Ask your water company for details of their policies and current rates. Their Customer Accounts Department may also be able to help you estimate levels of use.

Cleaning

Who is going to clean the premises, and what with? Is that in your service delivery staff's job descriptions? What about the toilets and kitchens?

If you employ cleaners, or contract a cleaning company how much are you going to pay them?

Refuse collection

Practices vary but some local authorities will want to levy a charge for the collection of non-domestic waste, or for the removal of large volumes or certain kinds of refuse. You may have to buy, lease or put a deposit on a wheeled bin. Or, ask them to waive such charges.

Renewals, redecoration, repairs and maintenance

Check the terms of your lease to determine your responsibility. Some leases contain re-decoration clauses at the end of lease term.

You must make a calculation based on condition of building, the kind of use it receives, any known problems, how much longer you intend to occupy.

The renewal of Capital items should be funded from your depreciation fund. They should not appear in the Revenue part of your calculations.

Fittings and furnishings

To determine the cost of fitting and furnishing premises start by drawing up a list of your requirements room by room, for example:

- *Entrance/Hallways*: signs, lighting, ramps, locks, entry-phone.
- *Reception*: carpet, chairs, noticeboard, receptionist desk, chair, staff/department pigeonholes.
- *Office*: room dividers, curtains/blinds, carpets, desks, chairs, visitor chairs, filing cabinets, lights, equipment tables, tea/coffee making space and store, noticeboards, staff lockers/coat-hanging space.

- *Other work spaces:* floor covering, work benches/equipment tables, seating, lighting, ventilation, cleaning materials and equipment.

- *Training/meeting room(s):* curtains/blinds, carpet, chairs, tables, flipchart, blackboard or similar; video & TV. Enough kettles, tea-cups and toilets for large meetings?

- *Play areas/creche:* carpet, smaller tables and chairs, play equipment, water supply/wet area/sink, children's toilets;

- *Kitchen:* cooker, fridge, freezer, food preparation areas, sinks, food storage, utensil storage;

- *Toilets:* fittings for adults, children & people with disabilities.

- *Storage:* stationery, other supplies and stocks, food, safe for money, deeds, other very high value items, secure equipment store; files (confidential and otherwise), library, archives.

You can exclude those items you have, and then draw up a shopping list of items to price, either new or secondhand, bought or leased. Even if you know that you can get some of them donated it is worth knowing what their value is. Most of the larger elements on this list – carpets, furniture, kitchen or office equipment – you may well want to count as capital expenditure, and depreciate accordingly (set aside money each year for their replacement when they wear out). It is also important to know the extent to which charitable donations are subsidising a contract service.

Finding out what things cost

If you want to find out how much an item costs you can ask two groups of people

- those who sell it
- those who have bought it.

If you just want to get a rough idea you can get away with

just asking someone from one group. But to cost accurately and economically you should find out both what others have paid (and if there are any hidden costs) before asking the seller what they would charge.

It can be difficult to get clear information from sales representatives about the price of an item. You just want information. They want to make a sale. You want to find out the price of the model that fits your specification. They want to sell the model on which they make the most profit – usually the top of the range. In fact they may really be trying to sell you not a piece of equipment but a leasing agreement or credit to finance the deal.

Tips

• Have a clear idea of what you want the product to do

• Be firm and assertive

• Decide on a line and stick to it e.g.

"I am costing our tender. There is no way we will go any further with buying one of these unless and until we win the contract."

"I do not have the authority to make an order on behalf of our organisation. I have to take a written quotation to my management committee."

"Our organisation had a bad experience with reps pressurising staff. My manager/Trustees will not buy from companies who keep ringing up. Don't call us we'll ring you."

"The terms of our trust prevent us from borrowing money." (this need not be true)

• If you are not sure what model you want ask for product particulars and a price list for a range of models

Buy or lease?

If you can afford the capital outlay you will generally find that it is much more economic to buy items outright than to lease them. There are exceptions:

- When you have a short-term need, or short term funding
- When you need to make only occasional use of an expensive piece of equipment or facility
- When maintaining the equipment or facility requires skills or resources you do not have or cannot spare

---

SETTING UP AN OFFICE – a checklist of things you may need

Stationery

Headed notepaper: Design of letterhead, typesetting and printing

Other printed stationery: envelopes, postcards business cards, compliments slips, invoices, membership cards, tickets, posters, maps

Photocopying paper
Continuous stationery for computers
Note pads
Envelopes
Message books,
Diaries and year-planners

Other consumable stationery items may include

Pens, pencils, felt-tips, note pads, files, binders, carbons, envelopes, padded envelopes notebooks, ribbons, correcting fluid, computer discs, dictating machine cassettes, sellotape, pins, clips, staples, ink,

Minor office equipment:

staplers, clock, key cupboard, cash-box, first aid tin, rulers, desk tidies, stationery racks, wastebins, postal scales, franking machine (large volumes of post only), paper trays, desk lamps, dust covers, noticeboards, ashtrays, fans, out of area telephone directories, dictionary etc

Filing system, – cabinets, locking drawers, concertina files, index tabs etc.

Shelving and filing of books, magazines etc

Cheapness, efficiency and economy

Contracts will place additional pressures on provider organisations to hold down their costs. In estimating the expenditure required to provide a service you should beware of making false economies, and always going for the cheapest option in purchasing equipment and assets.

In most contracts the biggest investment of money will be in staff. Depending on their pay scale, and the size of your overheads, employees could be costing your organisation anything from £8 to £20 an hour. You could be wasting a lot of money if, instead of getting on with delivering the service they are stuck on a bypass trying to coax an ancient vehicle back to life, or spending an afternoon a month addressing envelopes by hand.

Modern information technology – personal computers, faxes, answering machines – can greatly reduce the administrative burden on service staff and increase the productivity of managers and administrators in small organisations, provided that care is taken in purchasing and proper training is given to staff.

Telephones

You need to think about how many telephone lines and telephones you will need, and whether you will need some kind of system, either with or without a switchboard and someone to operate it. Modern systems offer considerable flexibility and ranges of features but the choice can be bewildering.

In selecting a system consider your future needs over the next 3-5 years as well as your immediate requirements. It may work out cheaper to start off with the skeleton of a more sophisticated system to which you can add as your needs grow. The volume of office telecommunications – for voice, fax and modem – is increasing dramatically.

Telephone costs, if a big factor, may now be broken down into a number of cost categories

- **Capital costs**
  Purchase of phones, exchange system, and any additional equipment – answering and fax machines
  Installation Charges
  VAT
- **Set Up Costs**
  Line Connection charges.
  VAT
- **Fixed Direct Costs**
  Rental of line, phones, exchange system or other equipment – quarterly in advance
  VAT
- **Depreciation of bought equipment**
  Annual maintenance contract, or a contingency for repair.
  VAT
- **Variable costs**
  The cost of calls and special services – quarterly in arrears
  VAT

Postage

Another cost of communicating with the outside world is postage. How many letters or parcels you send out, at first or second class rates, or as parcels, or using a courier service may be factors in your calculation (or they may be so small that they can be mentioned in a more general class). If you have no previous experience to base your calculation on, then you must make the best guess you can, monitor your performance, and revise accordingly. If you are sending out very large volumes of mail you can negotiate discounts from the post office. If you regularly post heavy packets to regular destinations investigate courier services. Monitor the relative cost of fax, data transmission and post. Remember to anticipate rises in the cost of postage for the period of operation.

Vehicles

- *Capital Costs:* remember that the capital costs of a vehicle are not necessarily restricted to the purchase price of the vehicle. There may be additional charges for some accessories, number plates or delivery. You may need to carry out some conversion work or adaptations – putting in a burglar alarm or wheelchair lift, or changing the seating. You may need to splash your name and logo (or your sponsor's) across the side of it. You should also consider secure garaging for the vehicle when not in use. You may save considerably on the revenue cost of insurance premiums if you can load setting up secure garaging onto a capital budget for vehicle purchase.

- *Revenue:* if your organisation has its own vehicles you will probably need to get a clear picture of the fixed and variable costs of running them. You may also need to apportion the costs of vehicles between different cost centres. If so you need some kind of log of use so that you can determine how much to charge to each contract.

You may find it convenient to establish a cost centre for revenue expenditure and income related to the vehicle and its use. You may need to include some or all of the following in your classes of expenditure.

- *Fixed Costs:*

  Lease payments
  Insurance
  Road fund Licence
  MOT
  Basic maintenance
  Subscription to recovery organisation
  Depreciation
  Garaging
  Salary and associated costs of driver, including PSV and HGV training.

Contingency:Hire of replacement vehicles in event of theft, accident etc

- *Variable Costs*

Petrol & Oil
Cleaning
Parking
Additional maintenance & repairs
Payments to casual drivers
Additional depreciation

Computers

This book can't offer you a detailed guide to buying computers. However, first time buyers of computers should bear the following points in mind.

Cost effective use of computers depends more on software than on hardware. Researching the right software, getting it properly installed and your staff or volunteers trained and confident in its use are essential steps, but they both cost money and time (which may be even more valuable to you). Choose a supplier who can give you the support you need. Make sure that the people who have to use the systems have enough time free from other commitments to get a thorough grasp of what they can do.

New uses will become apparent as you get to the know the technology and the systems. Only by having a computer will you find out value to your organisation of its various applications. However you may well find that word-processing – using the computer as a typewriter cum filing cabinet – can easily tie up one machine for most of the working day, so there isn't time for someone to get on the machine to do all the other jobs a computer could do, like run the desk top publishing programme and produce the newsletter, or build up a comprehensive database of clients, or do the accounts. Modern personal computers can be enormously powerful, fast and expensive. But still only one person can use one at a time. It may be better to buy two older machines with smaller memories, or slower running speeds.

Things to remember to cost

Set-up costs
Software
Computer(s)
Modem
Printer
Accessories (glare shields, mouse, dust covers, noise hoods etc)
Additional telephone lines – installation & rental
Secure location; desk, table, chair; appropriate lighting; secure back-up disc store.

Recurrent costs
Discs, Ribbons/cartridges, Paper.
E-mail subscriptions, Telephone charges
Cost of Staff Training
Loss of productive staff time during installation or upgrading
Insurance to cover the cost of replacing lost or damaged equipment and data
Maintaining Back-up systems
Maintenance & repair – contract
Depreciation

Consumables

In addition to assets you may also need to buy consumable items in order to supply a service. These will generally figure as variable costs, and may comprise a whole range of items (and classes of expenditure), depending on the nature of the service you are providing, and the equipment you deploy.

The sections on **Setting up an office** and **Computers** go through consumable items of stationery, discs, etc.

You should review all the activities of the users of your service, of your staff, volunteers, and management to identify all significant consumable items. Your list might include:

> Food and drink,
> Working clothing and laundry,
> Cleaning materials
> Bedding
> Toilet articles
> Film, video and audio tape,
> Batteries,
> Leaflets,
> Medical supplies,
> Art and craft materials,
> Raw materials for workshop production.

- How will you buy these? As needed? Bulk-buy in advance? What are the implications for cash-flow and VAT?

- Who will you buy them from? If from the contract purchasing authority you may wish to put the price you pay for such supplies onto the negotiating table.

- Where will you store such items? How will you exercise stock control to re-order in good time and avoid waste and pilfering? How will stock be distributed? Any transport costs? Do you need to insure stocks?

- Who is responsible for actually doing the buying and warehousing? How will that affect their productivity in respect of other tasks?

Depreciation

Depreciation means regularly setting aside money in order to replace capital purchases. It does not matter if your capital assets comprise two or three large value items or 20 smaller ones. It would be prudent, for example, if you buy 10 sewing machines at £350 each for a sewing workshop, to make allowance for their replacement when worn out.

How to work it out

You must make a judgement as to when items will need to be replaced. Equipment that is used heavily, for training purposes, or moved around a lot may need replacing more quickly.

Suppose you have bought a computer system for £9,000 on April 1st 1992. You expect to need to replace it at the end of three years. Under the simplest form of depreciation, called straight line depreciation you simply allow £3,000 a year for each of the three years 1992-93, 1993-94 and 1994-95.

You do this by showing that sum under the expenditure class Depreciation in your Income & Expenditure Account, and the same sum as income to a separate Capital Fund, which grows year by year to give you the money to buy a new system (a process sometimes called Capitalisation).

However it is sensible to make allowance for inflation, and calculate the likely price of the system when you need to buy it. In our example this will be at 1st April 1995. Thus, assuming prices of computer systems will rise by an average 7.5% over the next three years we can project the replacement cost thus:

at 1.4.1992 replacement is £9,000;
at 1.4.1993 it will be £9,675 (£9,000 x 1.075);
at 1.4.1994 it will be £10,400 (£9,675 x 1.075);
at 1.4.1995 it will be £11,181 (£10,400 x 1.075).

You can also use depreciation to make allowance for the re-sale or part-exchange value of your equipment should you find, say two years in, that you need to buy a more sophisticated system. The simplest way is to divide the final projected replacement cost of £11,181 between the three years on a straight line basis (£11,181/3=£3,727 per year).

For smaller sums there may be no point in making more precise projections.

But with larger amounts of money it is worth considering making allowance for a greater fall in the resale value of the items being depreciated in the early years. If, like cars, the secondhand value falls away sharply after 3 years, then distribute the depreciation accordingly.

Figure 4.1: DEPRECIATION – Some different ways of depreciating a £9,000 computer system

As in all costing exercises, make a full note of what your final figure represents.

	1992-3	1993-4	1994-5	**Fund total**
Straight line No inflation	3,000	3,000	3,000	**9,000**
Straight line Inflation 7.5% p.a.	3,727	3,727	3,727	**11,181**
Secondhand Value Inflation 7.5% p.a.	4,500	3,340	3,340	**11,180**

Lastly for large sums (tens or hundreds of thousands of pounds) you may wish to allow for the growth of the Capital Fund made by compounding interest. This is a complicated calculation for which you need to estimate future interest rates and apply them to your projected capital fund. This will then, of course, exceed your expected replacement cost. Unless you need to calculate the annual depreciation precisely you will be best off at this stage doing no more than making an estimate of the necessary reduction in the annual depreciation allowances to compensate.

Having decided on the staff costs for her proposed expansion – as she now found herself beginning to consider it – Morag turned to the costs of her office. She paid nothing for this, it came with use of the telephone, post system and so on of Social Services, and it had space for a second desk, which she could scrounge, but she would need a new filing cabinet. At first she thought that all she should put down was just £100 for the cabinet, but then she wondered about the position with Social Services. Would she be taking advantage of them by using the office for work, no matter how useful, that was in the area of a different Social Services office?

In the end she asked the Admin. Officer for a figure for the value of the office she used, and her access to the copier, switchboard etc. and put it down in the same proportions as before. The £100 for the filing cabinet was a problem; it would last for years, so it seemed wrong to put it down in the same way as, say, her own salary. In the end she just wrote it down separately at the bottom for the moment.

Munster Project – Costs

	Main Project	New Project
Salary (P/T Co-ordinator and P/T Assistant)	£9,000	£4,500
Premises/office costs (donated by SS)	£2,000	£1,000
One-off cost: Filing cabinet at		£100

(Continued on Page 88)

Chapter 5

Administration, management and other indirect costs

Administration, management and supervision costs

Take care in costing this area of activity. Most voluntary organisations have become so used to having inadequate management and administration that they underestimate the real indirect costs of providing quality services.

- Begin by making a list of everything that will have to be done (see Boxes)

- Then decide who is to do it

Do you need to take on extra staff? Don't forget their set-up costs – recruitment, induction, desk, chair etc.

- Then list the costs they will incur in doing it (e.g. phone, travel, office, supervision).

Check and revise your lists by going through all the administrative and management tasks that people in your organisation presently carry out and ask yourself what contribution they would make to the delivery of a service.

Taking on a contract may increase the number and kinds of

administrative and management tasks to be done in your organisation. It will probably result in your organisation's management committee, managers and other staff taking on more, and more serious responsibilities.

You should cost the contribution made by members of voluntary management committees. You may wish to carry out a valuation similar to that described for volunteers in Chapter 12. If they tender for, and take on the management of contract services they will certainly be involved in more work, and will probably need to acquire new and more sophisticated management skills.

- There may be a direct cost of training management committee members in budgeting and costing, or negotiation skills, or personnel management.

- There will certainly be more meetings; and higher photocopying and mailing costs. The management committee's expenses, such as phone calls or travel, may go up.

- If the contract requires considerable expansion a wholly voluntary management committee may simply not be able to cope with the additional workload on its own, and you may need to take on paid staff, either in a secretarial or administrative role, or as a delegated manager, or both.

Management tasks

A list to set you thinking about what your organisation may have to do to manage a contract

- Plan and review
- Develop policy
- Consult users
- Direct research
- Ensure equal opportunities in service delivery and employment

- Take responsibility for public monies.
- Establish financial management system for contracts
- Exercise financial planning and control
- Ensure that the organisation operates within the contract, the law, and in pursuit of its objectives.
- Recruit, support & supervise staff and volunteers
- Design work programmes, ensure performance and quality standards
- Prepare and implement Health and Safety policy
- Organise training for staff and volunteers
- Provide internal communications
- Design and implement Quality Assurance Systems
- Institute Monitoring
- Commission Evaluation
- Negotiation with Purchasers
- Negotiation with other Funders
- Prepare Reports for management committee
- Conduct Public Relations

Administration Tasks

A list to set you thinking about what your organisation may have to do to administer a contract

Financial Administration
- Book-keeping, and preparation of budgets, management accounts and annual accounts
- Invoicing
- Stock control and ordering
- PAYE/Payroll/Staff expenses
- Cash handling and banking

- VAT
- Internal Audit

Other administrative matters
- Secretarial and reception services – switchboard, post
- Booking resources
- Insurance
- Repairs and maintenance
- Liaison with legal advisers
- Servicing management committee
- Security
- Collection and collation of contract monitoring data
- Implement a health and safety policy
- Organise training for staff and volunteers
- Provide internal communications – bulletins, minutes, reports
- Circulate and direct information
- Produce reports
- Service management committee
- Service contract negotiations

Remember that the cost of your administrators and managers is not confined to their salaries plus national insurance and pension etc. They need somewhere to work from, they run up phone bills and travel expenses, their office equipment must be bought and depreciated or leased, and they need to be insured and trained and so on. Go back and work through Chapters 3 and 4, and the rest of this chapter and identify the staff, premises, equipment, and indirect costs you will incur in carrying out the management and administration of the contract.

Who manages?

Because administration and management has traditionally been under-funded, all sorts of people in voluntary organisations carry out management and administrative tasks:

- Management committee members (who may be volunteers, staff, or co-opted employees of another organisation)
- Volunteers
- Users
- Staff

This true even in organisations where there are also actual paid Managers (with a capital M) on distinct grades. Indeed voluntary organisations in which management becomes top-heavy, or divorced from service delivery may in fact rely more heavily on non-management staff to actually manage services, while the Managers manage each other.

Smaller organisations in particular should pay heed to the full costing of management, otherwise their staff and volunteers will in effect, be subsidising the purchasing authority.

If staff or volunteer time is being taken up by contract management you should cost that contribution, just as you should cost the salary of a contract manager.

How you do this will depend on your particular circumstances, but your options include these two:

- If staff are managing, you should ensure that their responsibilities are reflected in their job description and grade of pay.
- You could also pass the cost of management done by staff or volunteers on to the purchaser by reducing the level of a service for a given price. A project worker cannot spend one day a week on management tasks and provide five

days' worth of units of service. See Chapter 3 on **calculating available staff time**, and Chapter 7 on the **cost of quality**.

The cost of tendering

It may be very difficult for you to recoup the full cost of tendering for a contract from the contract price – and quite impossible if your bid is unsuccessful.

However it is in your interest to know how much the following cost:

- Preparatory work – such as staff and management time spent reading this book, researching how to supply a service, consulting users, and developing appropriate systems for quality assurance and monitoring, financial control and other management functions. These you would count as set-up costs.

- The actual negotiation of the contract, including time spent on correspondence and meetings, an allowance for the costs of travel, copying, telephone etc, and for secretarial/administrative back-up.

- Fees to professionals for advice or services in respect of the negotiation or tender – accountants, solicitor, other specialists or consultants.

These last two points, though connected to setting up each contract, are likely to recur throughout the run up to the renewal of every contract, and so I would incline towards counting them as recurrent costs.

- Remember that you may be able to recover the VAT on some set-up costs – if you are starting a contract service from scratch you may therefore recover some of your expenditure on legal fees etc. See Chapter 6 on **VAT**.

If your calculations for the above point to significant expenditure by your organisation in pursuit of a contract then you can press the purchaser for some reimbursement – charge them a higher price. The information you have produced may affect your decision to press ahead with tendering for this or other contracts.

Apportioning indirect costs

This is a tricky topic. Whatever method you use for apportioning Indirect costs someone is going to complain that they are not getting a fair deal. It may be service delivery staff and volunteers, who think that too much of the contract price is being creamed off to maintain the HQ. It may be administrators who want more recognition of their contribution, and a part-time book-keeper, please. And of course the purchasing authority may be suspicious that they are being asked to pay for some of the indirect costs of your organisation's other contracts and for its non-contract activities.

It is in your interest to arrive at a method of apportioning indirect costs which as accurately as possible reflects the reality of how resources are applied to different contracts and/or activities. In subsequent price negotiation you may wish to draw attention to, or away from how you have calculated the apportionment (see Chapter 12). You may want to manipulate the apportionment of indirect costs to cross-subsidise high priority but under-funded services, or to "seed" new developments. But for now you need to know what each contract is really costing you through indirect costs.

Job costing

Where labour or resources are simultaneously employed on several different contracts it is important to know how much is being applied to each.

Job Costing is the term used in manufacturing and other service industries to describe the systems used for this kind of monitoring.

Most voluntary sector managers are invariably doing several things at once, and it can be difficult – without a record – to recall how much time has been spent on a given project. In one week there might be a dozen phone calls, 5 or 6 follow-up letters, plus an afternoon on the costings and 3 meetings with staff, while in another week nothing. Hitherto very few voluntary organisations have used job costing methods, either because they have not been necessary, or because they are too disorganised to carry them out.

Nonetheless it will be more important for managers to keep a record of the work they do on each contract as contract funding grows.

Avoid complex or elaborate systems. Take a little time to choose appropriate categories – comprehensive but not too many. Staff enter the amount of time spent on each, at the end of the day (best) or at the end of the week (but no longer). Entries can be made in suitable units of time – hours, half days. It may be easier to set down an impression of the attention given to each during a day, expressed as a percentage. A simple database programme could collate and provide reports as required. But a note in the corner of each day's page of a diary will do as well.

Consider the position of the High Hopes Association, who run contracts for two local authorities. Contract A, with Loamshire County Council, brings in £75,000. Contract B, on the other hand, with Coketown Borough Council, brings in only £25,000, but involves complex negotiation and very careful management. It therefore takes up 50% of the Development Manager's time, 65% of the Finance Manager's time, and even 25% of the Chief Executive's time. If the officers of the Association don't know what proportion of management time is being spent on Contract B how can they negotiate a higher price or higher management cost allowance from Coketown Council?

Using a central cost centre

You should consider setting up a Central cost centre, against which all management and administration costs, and other shared indirect costs are charged, and which receives income from contract cost centres according to a clear formula, or set of formulae.

Figure 5.1: CENTRAL COST CENTRE

Expenditure

Salaries

Organiser	15,570	Scale point 30
Administrator	6,159	Scale point 23; half time
National Insurance	2,181	at 10.45% (Organiser), 9% (Administrator)
Pay Award	978	at 6% from July 1st
Total salaries	**24,888**	
Organiser travel	350	
Office expenses	250	
Telephone	600	
Rent	1,000	
Depreciation	300	Office equipment £1500 / 5 years
Accountant & Audit	345	
Total expenditure	**27,733**	

Income

Contract X	6,933	25% central staff time = 25% contribution to costs
Contract Y	13,867	50% central staff time = 50% contribution to costs
Grant	7,000	
Total income	**27,800**	

Figure 5.2: A LARGER CENTRAL COST CENTRE

Cost centre	01 Central	Notes
Central staff salaries		
General Secretary	18,375	Scale point 36
Contracts Manager	16,545	Scale point 32
Finance Manager	17,040	Scale point 33
Admin Assistant	13,563	Scale point 26
National Insurance	6,847	at 10.45%
Pension	3,276	at 5%
Redundancy fund	655	at 1%
Pay award	2,949	say 6% from 1st July
Total salary costs	79,250	
Management committee	250	Members' expenses
Staff travel	750	
Staff training	1,200	Four courses at £300
Telephone	1,750	Rental and calls on two lines
Postage	500	
Photocopying	200	37.3% share of Photocopier cost centre
Stationery	300	
Publicity	800	Annual Report £500, AGM £75, £225 member/funder leaflet
Occupancy (share)	1,500	33.5% share of Occupancy cost centre
Depreciation	1,667	Fittings of £10,000 / 15 years; office equipment £5,000 / 5 years
Insurance	450	Employers, Bldgs, Contents, Public liability for HQ, central staff only
Accountant & Audit	590	
Legal fees	450	Contracts scrutiny
Subscriptions	250	
Library	250	
Total expenditure	90,157	

Figure 5.2 continued

Income

Other cost centres

Contracts:

02 Day centre	9,016	10% central staff time = 10% contribution to costs
03 Outreach	22,539	25% central staff time = 25% contribution to costs
04 Special programme	22,539	25% central staff time = 25% contribution to costs
This cost centre 01:		
Subscriptions	3,063	Last year's members renewing at new rates
Donations	12,500	Slawkenburgius Trust
Grant	20,000	Core funding from Central Govt (Dept of Convenience).
Fees	500	Talks, training
Total income	**90,157**	

Figure 5.1 illustrates the position in many smaller organisations – where, for example the entire management and administration team consists of one and a half people. The central cost centre bears all their salary costs, their travel, the costs of their small office, phone, rent and depreciation, and lastly their accountant's fee for services and audit. They spend 75% of their time on contract work; for their other work they receive a grant of £7,000. They apportion the indirect costs of their contracts on a blanket percentage basis. So cost centre X takes up 25%, and Cost centre Y 50% of the total expenditure of the central cost centre, and so they contribute to the income accordingly.

Figure 5.2 shows a larger central cost centre for a larger organisation. The detail may suggest some items you need to include in your costings.

In large contracts the purchaser may want a detailed breakdown of indirect costs. This is probably the prelude to an argument about how they are allocated. If pressed show them budgets with classes consolidated to obscure minor items they may object to paying for. Quote the AMA's guidance (see end of chapter). As far as possible resist different methods of apportioning for different contracts. Apart from anything else the extra management and book-keeping time required adds to the indirect costs without producing a single extra unit of provision.

Other indirect costs

Insurance

Many voluntary sector managers have difficulty with insurance. It can be complicated, and expensive; it can also be easily trimmed or lost altogether in budgeting without anyone noticing... until something goes wrong. That is too late to find out that inadequate or non-existent insurance can put a voluntary organisation out of business.

There are many different kinds of insurance, and you should review your organisation's needs with a competent insurance broker. Choose one that is experienced in commercial or public sector insurance, not one that handles your car insurance. You may also get useful advice on your insurance needs from the purchasing authority's legal department. The contract is likely to require you to "maintain adequate insurance cover", or words to that effect, and it is worth knowing exactly what is meant by that.

Without a helpful broker it can be difficult to get any indication of the likely cost of cover without actually applying for it. This may involve completing long and complex forms, full of hard-to-answer questions. Insurance companies want to assess the risk before they quote a premium (price). The greater they perceive the risk to be, the higher the premium.

The insurance you need will depend on the nature of your organisation and its activities. However if you employ staff the law demands that you should have Employers' Liability Insurance. Many policies extend cover to volunteers as well.

The following will also be essential to all but the very smallest organisations:

- *Public liability*
- *Personal accident* or *injury* (to staff, volunteers, management committee members)
- *Loss or damage* to assets either on specified premises (Contents) or anywhere else (All Risks).

You should also consider your need for:

- *Buildings insurance* – essential if you own one
- *Insurance for stocks* of supplies
- *Motor insurance* – for volunteer drivers as well as your vehicles
- *Professional indemnity* – against giving wrong advice
- *Money insurance* – expensive but may be worth it if you deal in a lot of cash
- *Fidelity bond* – Insuring for the honesty of staff
- *Life assurance* and *medical insurance* either as a benefit for staff, or to compensate for the loss of key staff.
- *Loss of profits insurance* (in addition to a *contents/all risks policy*) to pay for the reconstruction of records, loss of income etc
- *Legal insurance*

Packages of policies tend to offer better value than a collection of single policies – but only if the portfolio they offer meets your needs. Insurance costs may increase dramatically if you make a lot of claims, or move to what the insurance company sees as a high risk area (anywhere in the inner cities, for example)

You may find that a policy will be offered subject to security or fire prevention measures (Locks, alarms, sprinklers) being introduced, all of which will cost money (both materials and labour).

More indirect costs

If you have not included them elsewhere you should also make allowance for the following:

- *Bank charges.* Most banks now charge non-personal accounts for ordinary transactions like cheques, credits, transfers and standing orders. Systems of charging vary greatly; it may well be worth shopping around to find a charging structure that suits your needs. Ask bank managers for their estimate of what their charges would be on your account. It doesn't harm to ask for free – or reduced rate – banking as the bank's donation to your good cause.

These bank charges are quite separate from any interest charges which you may have to pay on any bank loans or overdraft facilities. But remember that ordinary bank charges may be increased to a higher rate if you run your account into the red.

- *Legal costs.* You should obtain a legal opinion on all but the simplest proposed contracts before signing; you may also need a solicitor's services if you enter into a lease for premises.

- *Accountants' fees* (including annual audit, advice on contracting, new systems and due proportion of annual audit costs).

- *Fees of other professional advisers:* (chartered surveyors, architects, management consultants etc) whose work is connected to the contract.

- *Information and publicity.* You may need to promote a service and/or your organisation in order to attract users, staff, volunteers, or additional funding. You may also need to keep these same groups of people informed via annual reports, bulletins, press coverage etc.

- *Contingency.* It is prudent to include a contingency allowance to give the organisation a measure of protection organisation will face greater demands on its reserves. Make sure that you have adequate reserves for both the new contract and for your other areas of activity.

Finally

The Association of Metropolitan Authorities in its document *"Contracts for Social Care"* recommends that "Local authorities should consider directly providing or paying for training, administration, premises, equipment, legal or financial advice, transport, etc."

A word of caution however; sending staff on a training course at the local authority's expense is fine; using the local authority with whom you have a contractual agreement as your source of legal advice creates a clear conflict of interest.

Morag >> *a continuing story* (from Page 73)

Morag considered what extra costs there would be if she took on the new work. She divided all her present costs into just two headings, Administration and Club/Volunteer costs. She could always extend the sheet again, as she had started keeping a note, on another sheet, of exactly how she had arrived at each figure. For the new project, as it would be just half the size of the old on and in the absence of anything better to go on, she just put 50% of her present costs.

One other thing was the cost of the time in doing just this preparatory thinking. Having heard the Admin. Officer say that his time cost about £10 an hour, she used the same figure for herself, made an heroic guess, and added another £200 at the bottom of her page:

Munster Project – Costs

	Main Project	New Project
Salary (P/T Co-ordinator and P/T Assistant)	£9,000	£4,500
Premises/office costs (donated by SS)	£2,000	£1,000
One-off cost: Filing cabinet at		£100
Contract preparation at £10/hr		£200

(Continued on Page 105)

Chapter 6
VAT and other taxes

This chapter aims to give you initial guidance on costing any liability for taxes your organisation may incur through taking on a contract. I am indebted to Sandy Adirondack and Richard Macfarlane for much of the material used here. For a fuller (and admirably concise) explanation of VAT, and a useful summary of how charitable and legal status affects tax liability in taking on a contract I strongly recommend their companion volume in the Contract Culture Series "Getting Ready For Contracts".

You should also take detailed advice from an accountant with experience in tax matters as they apply to charities and companies, as the tax regulations are complex, and vary considerably according to the legal status of your organisation, the nature of the service you are providing, and the kinds of expenditure and income you deal with.

If an organisation has charitable status it is exempt from income tax (though its employees, of course, are not), corporation tax and capital gains tax. If it does not have charitable status then you should take advice, as the permutations of the different types of legal status are too complex to describe here. Rate reliefs for charitable and non-charitable organisations are described above in the section on premises in Chapter 4.

VAT

Everyone – whether an individual, a business or an organisation – pays VAT on most goods and services which they buy. No-one is exempt from having to pay VAT.

But if a business or organisation is registered for VAT, it can usually reclaim the VAT it has paid out. It does this by offsetting the VAT it has collected against the VAT it has paid out. If it has collected more than it has paid out, it sends the difference to HM Customs and Excise; if it has paid out more VAT than it has collected, it gets a payment from Customs and Excise.

An organisation which is not registered for VAT cannot reclaim the VAT it has paid out (nor can it charge it to anyone else !).

So why doesn't every organisation register for VAT? You may find that you have no choice and have to register whether you want to or not. If you are supplying goods and services to a value above the VAT threshold (£36,000 in 1992-3) in any 12-month period then you must register. You can register below that level but you should carefully weigh the advantages and disadvantages with your accountant before doing so.

The principal disadvantage for most voluntary organisations is that once registered for VAT you must charge it to everyone to whom you supply goods or services. Though there are exemptions you may have to charge VAT to your users or members (who can't reclaim it) as well as to a contract purchasing authority (which can).

Services provided under a contract will almost certainly be classed as business activities for VAT purposes, but may well be exempt from VAT. For charitable organisations exemption will depend on the nature of the goods or services provided, who they are supplied to, and whether the activity is being run "for profit" or "otherwise than for profit". These are judgements that will be made by the VAT inspectors, not you or the contract purchasing authority. Don't take risks with VAT.

Sometimes it can be more advantageous for the activity to be chargeable to VAT, sometimes for it to be exempt. It is vital to get proper financial advice and sort this out before submitting costings for a contract to a purchasing authority.

VAT regulations as a whole are fairly complex; those relating to charities and voluntary organisations are no exception. Your local VAT office (see under "Customs" in the phone book) can supply general information and a range of specific free leaflets on how VAT applies to charities, clubs and associations, and to certain activities like training, printed matter and catering. You must read the relevant leaflets, and discuss how taking on a contract will affect your liability for VAT with your accountant or auditor. If necessary you can get clarification of the regulations as they apply to your organisation from your local VAT office.

The consequences of VAT registration for costing

- If you register for VAT you will have to change your book-keeping system. VAT input tax (the tax you pay on goods and services you buy) and VAT output tax (the tax you charge to those who buy your services) must each be recorded in separate columns or as separate classes in your book-keeping system. So you must deduct the VAT element from invoices and cash expenditure before entering the cost, exclusive of VAT, in the appropriate class.

- VAT input tax and VAT output tax should not appear in your Income and Expenditure Account; it's not your income or expenditure; you are merely handling it for the government.

- For this reason your financial projections should also exclude VAT (except for the cash-flow projection – see below). That means when drawing up an Income and Expenditure budget (see Chapter 8) you must set down costs at prices without VAT, and income without any VAT component that may be added on to the value of sales, or to a contract.

• Take particular care in using figures from pre-registration days as the basis for estimating future costs.

There are two categories of goods and services for which you may wish to include the VAT inputs in your financial projections because there is no VAT output to cancel them out. You would then have a cost to you which should be shown in your Income and Expenditure Account.

Exempt supplies

A significant number of goods and services supplied by charities and other voluntary organisations are exempt from VAT provided that the charge (as fees to users or as a charge to another body) does no more than cover the cost, including overheads, of providing the goods or service. This is what is meant in VAT terms, by making supplies "otherwise than for profit".

Examples of exempt supplies include the "provision of care, treatment or instruction to elderly, sick, distressed or disabled people", the protection of children and young people, education, training and retraining, and some provision for under-5's.

Because you cannot charge VAT on exempt supplies, you cannot generally reclaim the VAT which you pay out in making those supplies. This will not be very important if VAT payments concerned are small; but at the current VAT rate (1991-92) of 17.5% you could build up a substantial deficit on your VAT account if for example you have to buy petrol, hire equipment, or make lots of telephone calls or consume other VATable supplies in order to provide the service.

Zero rated supplies

Books, children's clothing, and certain supplies made to and by charities for blind people or medical charities are among the list of zero-rated items. VAT is chargeable on zero-rated supplies, but at a rate of 0%. So if you are supplying zero-rated services or goods you will not have to charge anything extra to the individuals or organisations who pay for whatever you are supplying.

Zero-rated supplies are not exempt from VAT, however. The distinction is that their value counts towards the VAT threshold; that of exempt supplies does not.

Because zero-rated supplies are VATable you can reclaim the VAT which you pay out in the course of making those supplies.

VAT and cash flow

Though you must keep VAT out of your Income & Expenditure Account, in both statements and budgets, VAT will affect you cash flow, and you must include it in your rolling forecast. How you do this is demonstrated in Chapter 9.

Chapter 7
The Cost of Quality

including equal opportunities, monitoring and evaluation

The "Contract Culture" is supposed to be about quality services. Documents from central and local government, academics and voluntary sector commentators abound with frequent references to the importance of quality assurance and quality monitoring. However quality is not to be secured without some cost.

This section looks at the kinds of expenditure you may have to incur in order to secure quality. This is so that you can ensure that you build in to your calculations the real cost of providing a service to the quality standards specified in the contract, and of implementing the quality assurance and monitoring mechanisms also specified or implied. It also explores the relationship between quality, volume and price and provides a method of calculating a volume of service for a given cost and quality.

The theory of **Total Quality Management** or TQM insists that such practices – and therefore the cost of them – are an integral part of your whole operation. Quality is not an afterthought, a post-facto add-on. Nonetheless it is crucial that you do understand very clearly (a) what elements give the required quality to the service and (b) what those elements cost. In the event of the purchaser offering an inadequate price for a service, the cost of quality will become the very fulcrum of negotiation. You need to know the consequences of compromise for you, your users, for the purchaser, and for levels and standards of service.

The issue is one that has been recognised by the Association of Metropolitan Authorities in their guidance "Quality and Contracts in the Personal Social Services":

> "Authorities need to recognise that the sharpening of aims and objectives and the inclusion of quality clauses in contracts has highlighted the fact that often the funding available has not always allowed voluntary organisations to deliver services of the quality which both they and the department desire. The level or quality of service has therefore had to be reduced from that originally anticipated."

The main cost of quality in social care services is in staff time. We may consider this under five headings:

1. development of service and quality systems;

2. service delivery staff;

3. administrative & support staff;

4. supervisors and managers;

5. staff motivation and responsibility.

1. Development of the service and quality assurance systems

You may here need to include the initial cost of researching similar services in other areas; the time spent on defining and developing quality standards; the time and other costs of securing service user involvement; and evolving and maintaining the quality assurance system.

2. Service delivery staff

You will need to be sure that your estimates of the amount of time staff or volunteers need to do the job to the required standard are realistic. Does the service specification make any requirements for contact ratios, client/hours, rest periods, or case-loads? Are these requirements themselves mutually compatible and realistic? What margins do you need to add for the practical management of the service.

If the service is a new one you may well wish to negotiate a specific review of staffing levels and the service specification into the contract.

An essential component of any quality assurance system is adequate supervision and support for staff and volunteers. That is likely to mean something like opportunities for discussion with peers, and regular one to one meetings with a supervisor, and an open door for emergencies. See indirect/management support costs below.

What training will your staff or volunteers need in order to provide a service to the required quality? It may be that your present staff and volunteers require none or very little. That may well be because you have already spent money on their training, or as is the case in many voluntary groups, the quality of their work comes from their experience with your organisation. But if they leave what are the costs of getting new recruits to perform to the required standard? Will you have to buy-in training at short notice? Or redeploy more senior staff back into service delivery?

3. Administrative and support staff

They also have a role to play in assuring quality. In the past many voluntary organisations have got by with remarkably few administrative assistants, receptionists, book-keepers, cleaners and so on, The work has been done on a rota, or by the first person to pick up the phone, or mainly by volunteers with staff filling the gaps in an ad-hoc manner.

You must now ask yourself whether such improvised arrangements allow you to fulfil the service specification to the required standard. What if the standard is "right first time, every time"? Can you rely on anybody who happens to be on hand to answer the phone and put the caller through to the right team? Have you made provision either for taking on extra staff, or made due allowance in existing staff job descriptions or in volunteers' duties?

Does taking on a contract mean either a substantial change in the nature, or a disproportionate increase in the volume of administrative and support tasks? What training do administrative and support staff need?

4. Managers

The burden of quality assurance falls heavily on managers. As we have seen the introduction of a contract or service agreement may impose additional demands on the limited management resources of many voluntary organisations, of which quality assurance is one.

You will wish to ensure that supervisors and managers have workloads which allow them (a) time to undertake regular supervision sessions with all staff who report to them and (b) time to take any action arising from those sessions. Have you got enough supervisors and managers?

Do your supervisors and managers have the necessary skills for quality management? How much will it cost to train them – both in course fees and other expenses, and in cover for their absences on courses?

5. Motivation and responsibility

The motivation of your staff and volunteers is absolutely crucial to providing a quality service. But it cannot be directly purchased. It can be nurtured, often at little or no additional expense; or it may be simply neglected; or it may be inadvertently damaged by over zealous cost control. In particular you should beware of sacrificing this precious asset in order to make small economies.

Some directly costable material factors undoubtedly influence staff motivation: levels of pay, terms and conditions of employment; security of employment. Investing management time in a formal staff appraisal system can help. But in a sector that generally calls for a high level of personal commitment from workers (whether paid or voluntary) less quantifiable factors are also important, and you should consider the following:

- Job satisfaction and workloads: You should review the balance of tasks you are asking each staff member and volunteer to undertake. Are some isolated in specialised and unrewarding corners? You must also appraise the volume of work and the stress entailed. If a contract means expanding your operations then you cannot afford to let key workers burn themselves out in the first few months. That goes for managers and supervisors as well as the people doing the face to face care work. You may conclude as a result that you need more staff or volunteers to perform a given set of functions, and/or more supervisors and support staff to help them do it.

- A sense of responsibility usually accompanies a sense of ownership and control. These are only acquired through some sort of involvement in decision-making. This is exactly the kind of time-consuming activity which makes voluntary organisations uncompetitive commercially. Many voluntary organisations have strong traditions of self-management; many volunteers and project staff groups have taken on responsibilities and earned considerable autonomy for themselves. All of this contrasts with much of the private sector, where managers are accustomed to imposing decisions. If you feel that how your organisation works is integral to the quality of service it provides then make sure that your costings allow you to continue in that way.

- Staff are more likely to commit themselves to a service if the organisation is able to offer them some form of longer-term commitment – opportunities to develop skills and experience, and progress through a career structure, for example. Can you build a quality service on staff who can only afford to do the job for a couple of years?

Other costs of assuring quality

These are associated with premises and the physical environments in which staff work and users receive services; and with the necessary plant, equipment and materials. These have been examined in Chapter 4.

You should review these resources asking yourself the following questions:

- What contribution should it make to a quality service?
- Does it do the job to the standard that will be required of them under the contract?
- Can it do it reliably and consistently for the life of the contract?
- Is it free of commitments to other non-contract uses?

If the answer to any of these last three is "no" then you need to consider what the costs would be of replacing or supplementing these assets to ensure the required quality.

The cost of equal opportunities

Putting an equal opportunities policy into effect can cost money. This section aims to help you anticipate additional expenditure and build it into your contract price. Equal opportunities are the kind of quality consideration which will have implications for all costs – indirect as well as direct.

The cost of consultation

Involving disadvantaged groups in policy-making – implicit in any customer care policy – may entail costs, both in terms of staff-time and in such incidental items as translation of documents, hiring rooms, etc.

A local authority education department wanted to consult with deaf children and their parents, and with deaf people who had been through the education system. Because this group had never been consulted before some staff time was needed to make contacts and encourage participation. A series of meetings were set up between the parents and deaf people, and the Chief Education Officer and other senior officers. Invitations, agendas and minutes were prepared in large print. The Education Authority's presentation was presented on overhead projector acetates designed on an Apple Mac computer, and copies of the overhead projector acetates were sent out in advance. For the meetings themselves a British Sign language Interpreter was employed, and on one occasion an Induction Loop system installed.

Recruitment

Do you need to prepare advertising or other material in other languages? If so translation, checking, typesetting/ artwork and printing costs must be considered. Advertising posts more widely, or through specialist media aimed at under-represented groups will be more expensive.

Translation of printed material into other languages will require the translation itself, new typesetting and artwork, and proof-reading – checking style and cultural tones as well as spelling and punctuation. Consider carefully how much and what kind of material needs translation. Take local advice on the specific languages and dialects used by ethnic minority communities in your area.

You need also to consider the costs of reaching people with sensory disabilities – e.g. using braille, cassettes, large print text, British Sign Language interpreters, induction loop system.

Child care

Budgeting for the costs of child care can be difficult,

particularly for small organisations, or when the number and ages of children to be cared for may vary. Here are three options:

- **"In-house"** nursery/creche, requiring staff (as sub-contractors, full time or sessional staff), premises, equipment, toilets, kitchens, etc.

- **subsidised places** at other creche/nursery. Under this arrangement you will almost certainly have to pay a premium to reserve places

- helping parents make their **own arrangements** and paying their child-care expenses to a predetermined ceiling, per parent. Using a recognised rate – like that of the National Childminders Association – may be helpful.

CALCULATING CHILD CARE COSTS

For a course of 6 half-day training sessions for up to 12 volunteer advice workers.

- Allow £1.25 per hour for 1st child, x 4 hours per session x 6 sessions = £30 per for every first child for the whole course.

- Allow 75p per hour for every subsequent child in a family x 4 x 6 = £18 for every subsequent child in a family for the whole course.

You must now estimate how many children will require care, by canvassing prospective students, looking at past courses and or simply making the best guess you can.

In this case you think that there are unlikely to be more than 3 parents with child care commitments, and not more than 6 children between them - say 3 x 1st children @ £30 each, and 3 x second children @ £18 each = £144.

As a preliminary estimate, this is good enough. You should know before the course begins if the guess on numbers is too high or low, and can either spend the surplus on something else, or take steps to raise further funds to cover the deficit.

Access

The costs of making many older buildings fully accessible to disabled people, and to children in prams and push chairs can be very high. If access is a central part of your quality standard then you must negotiate paying for it with the purchaser. If you can't afford to do it all, then you can still do some. Begin by taking advice from people with experience: disabled people's organisations, local authority Equal Opportunities Units, Department of Employment Disablement Resettlement Officers. Draw up a prioritised list of measures that need to be taken, and cost them. If you can't do them all at once, plan a realistic programme to implement them year by year.

The importance of taking advice in this field cannot be too strongly emphasised. You do not want to waste money on architect's or builders' fees to create solutions from scratch, when tried and tested plans or products are available off the shelf.

You also want to ensure that your organisation – or your purchaser – makes full use of any grant aid that may be available for capital or conversion work.

Most of the costs associated with creating access will be capital or set-up costs. In any building or conversion work it will work out much cheaper if access requirements are included in the specification at an early stage.

The cost of monitoring

Monitoring is intended as a protection against default. It should protect users and purchasers against poor quality services, and providers against loss of contract.

Many voluntary groups have no experience of systematic monitoring. Beware of collecting unnecessary data. Not only does it waste money, it also obscures useful information. Monitoring arrangements specified in a contract should be carefully scrutinised to understand the time and expense involved for your organisation. Press the purchaser for as tight a definition of the aim of the monitoring exercise as possible. Then – and only then – should you look for the most cost-effective means of achieving it.

Here are key questions on costing monitoring:

- What information is required, and when, by the purchaser?
- What information is required, and when, by the provider?

The answers to these two questions may not be the same.

- Who will collect data and when?
- How will it be recorded?
- Who will collate and process it?
- Who – within the service provider organisation – will review it?
- How much staff time – at what grades – will be required?
- Will they need training to do it?
- Will they need computer support to do it? What hardware and software will you use?

It may be that the required monitoring can be achieved through minor adjustments to existing staff reporting procedures; that supervisors and managers merely add another question or two to their regular supervision sessions and paragraph to their reports. But what if your organisation does not have that kind of structure in place? Or, as is the case in many organisations – that structure is in place, but is desperately under-resourced and stretched to the limits?

If user or customer's views on the service delivered need to be gathered then you need to consider who is to do it.

- If staff, what impact will that have on the service delivered – both in quantitative and qualitative terms?
- if manager/supervisors, what about their workloads?
- if you bring in external monitors, what will they charge in fees and other expenses?

The cost of evaluation

Evaluation differs from monitoring. Monitoring collects and collates information about a service; it looks at what goes into providing a service. Evaluation interprets information, and arrives at judgements about how far outcomes meet the policy objectives of a service.

But from a costing point of view the same sorts of considerations must be born in mind. Who is going to do it? How much time will it take them? How much training and support do they need? Can you modify existing structures, or do you need to start from scratch? Remember that if the exercise is to have any point the lessons of evaluation must be worked back through your management or support systems into the provision of service.

While some evaluation may be carried out "in-house" (and implementing its findings certainly must be) it may be more appropriate to hire external evaluators. If you and the purchasing authority agree on this then make sure their costs are reflected in the contract price.

An important factor is the need to involve service users in evaluation. This will incur staff time costs, and additional expenses.

One thing Morag very much wished to build into her costings was some form of evaluation. The original project had been part of a professional research project, and was known to be effective for children chosen by teachers using a carefully designed check-list procedure.

Would the same check-list be valid when used by Health Centre staff? She couldn't be sure. So she rang the original developer of the project, Sally Dunne, at the Polytechnic (where she was now Head of Department, as well being on Morag's management committee) and asked her if a very simple evaluation could be done as a student's postgraduate research project. Sally was happy to agree, but suggested they should at least try putting on £1,000 for the costs of this. Morag added another heading:

Munster Project – Costs

	Main Project	New Project
Salary (P/T Co-ordinator and P/T Assistant)	£9,000	£4,500
Premises/office costs (donated by SS)	£2,000	£1,000
Administration costs	£825	£412
Club and volunteer costs	£2,380	£1,190
Evaluation		£1,000
One-off cost: Filing cabinet at		£100
Contract preparation at £10/hr		£200

(Continued on Page 128)

PART 2

Marshalling the Information

In the preceding section we have looked at what must be costed, and how figures for costs may be obtained or calculated. In this section we will be looking at how those figures can be marshalled to make useful projections.

Chapter 8
Drawing up a budget

This chapter explains:

- How cost centres are brought together in an Income and Expenditure Budget;
- How such budgets for different cost centres are inter-related
- How such budgets can be projected over several years

Income and expenditure account

The **Income and Expenditure Account** is the record of all transactions that relate to a given period. So in addition to the money received and paid out during that period (which on its own is called a **Receipts and Payments** account) you may need to include the appropriate proportion of other payments and receipts, made before or after, but which relate to that period.

In the private sector an Income and Expenditure Account is often referred to as a Profit and Loss Account.

An Income and Expenditure budget or projection is a statement of all the income and expenditure for an organisation – or just a cost centre – that you anticipate for a given period.

You have to decide what period the budget is for. The simple answer is the duration of the contract. If you are costing an ongoing service, or a longer term contract then you will need to draw up a detailed Income and Expenditure budget for the first year of operation, and to make projections for subsequent years. Obviously you cannot be as confident about events in three year's time as you can about next year's performance. A rolling three year budget therefore, offers detailed view of the immediate future (first year) and maps out the main features for years 2 and 3; it can be updated and rolled forward each year.

Unless your start date coincides with the start of your financial year (usually April 1) you may later have to divide a single year operational year budget between two financial years budgets for the purposes of financial management.

It can be very helpful in preparing and analysing an I&E budget to include a column showing recent actual figures for the activity, if available and relevant. This enables comparisons to be easily made. If this year's figures will be the most helpful then quarter or half-year results may, with care, be projected forward to produce a set of full year results.

A small organisation, on a small contract, may be able to operate just on a Receipts and Payment Account, and do without income and expenditure accounting and separate cash flow.

Traditional budgeting – The process

Many organisations in the voluntary sector use the following budgetary formula:

Take what we spent last year
Add 10% "for inflation" and fiddle the figures around a bit till they come out neatly and balance
Bung in a grant application
Get what we got last year plus 2% for inflation
Carry on spending roughly what we spent last year
Panic when something goes wrong.

This broadly historical method of costing and budgeting has its advantages – notably it saves a lot of work. The main disadvantage is that it allows costs to rise without necessarily increasing resources where they are most needed.

The "clean sheet" budgeting alternative

This method, by contrast, starts each year's budgeting with an explicit specification of the activity to be costed but a blank sheet so far as the actual costs are concerned. The objective is to meet the specification at the minimum cost. Managers, management committee members, staff and volunteers may all find the that such an approach threatens considerable upheaval and disruption. "Clean sheet" budgeting can only be successfully undertaken with a thorough knowledge of how the service concerned is delivered, and of how that incurs costs.

In trying to re-design the service on paper to meet the specification, (instead of copying what was done last year) you may straighten out some inefficiencies but in the process destroy those nuances and traditions which have grown up over time and which give the service its quality. For example it may appear a waste of expensive staff time for a qualified therapist to drive the minibus once a week; in fact it gives her a chance to talk informally to volunteers and users.

Conversely you may find that staff or volunteers feel liberated and recharged with motivation if time-honoured but inefficient practices are removed, perhaps freeing up money for a needed piece of equipment in the process.

Consultation with service delivery staff and volunteers is a key part of the budgeting process. Usually the people who actually do a job have plenty of ideas on how to do it more cost effectively. In too many organisations – voluntary, statutory and private – no-one bothers to ask them. In many voluntary groups, of course, the people who deliver the service are also the people who have to draw up the budgets.

Budgeting from the bottom up

In budgeting you need to begin at the bottom and work your way up.

- Start by putting figures to individual classes of expenditure and income in each cost centre

- Bring all the cost centres together and check their inter-relationships.

- Only when you have a picture of the whole organisation's projected expenditure can you forecast the cash flow and calculate the working capital you need.

- You may then need to revise your budgets to meet the extra cost of borrowing working capital.

- You will also need to make other revisions before you can move on from costing (working out what a service will cost you to provide) to pricing (working out how much to charge for providing it).

You need to start budgeting early. Consultation across the organisation, and down to service delivery staff and volunteers can take a long time; so can researching costings, co-ordinating different cost centres and working out budgets.

You may need to start work on individual cost centre budgets in September/October if you are to have a complete budget by Christmas, so that you can begin serious price negotiation with the purchaser in January for a contract to start on the 1st of April.

Budgeting – the paper

You will save considerable time by preparing a blank budget form, first on paper, and then, if you wish, as a template spreadsheet file. Figure 8.1 gives an example. A header section reminds the reader that it contains confidential information, and identifies the piece of paper by:

Contract name and code number
Cost centre number

It also specifies the period for which the budget has been drawn up;

The number and date of this draft

Who has prepared it

Who has checked it or approved it

The main section of the form provides lines or rows to list down the page the classes of expenditure and income, and columns across the page corresponding to successive years, different cost centres or to compare different options within a single year.

Figures are totalled vertically and horizontally to check arithmetic as well as give totals for each row (class of expenditure over x years or in all cost centres) and for each column (classes of expenditure/income in that year or cost centre).

There is also space for comments on each line. This is the all-important space for you to note down the assumptions on which the figure is based. If the space is not big enough use numbers to refer to the appropriate note on an attached sheet.

Filling in the form

Round pence up or down to the nearest pound. The rule is 50p and over – round up; 49p and under – round down. So £5.52 becomes £6; and £9.42 becomes £9.

Take care to align units, tens and hundreds and thousands to avoid errors in totting up.

Use a pencil and rubber, inking over only when you have completed the entire budget to your satisfaction (which works fine) or use a spreadsheet program on your computer.

Make notes of the assumptions used as you go.

Figure 8.1: BLANK BUDGET FORM

INCOME AND EXPENDITURE BUDGET *CONFIDENTIAL*

Cost Centre: Contract prepared by: Period

Draft No./Date   Checked:

Cost centre or year	(a)	(b)	(c)	(d)	(e) Total a+b+c+d	Comments
Total Expenditure						

INCOME						
Total Income						
Balance						Total income less total expenditure

114

Completing a cost centre budget

Go through your specification (and read Chapters 3 to 7) and list the costs you will occur in meeting it, under the following headings:

- Capital costs
- Set up costs
- Fixed direct costs
- Variable direct costs
- Indirect costs

You must now make specific calculations of costs and enter them line by line on your form. It is usually more convenient to keep your capital budget quite separate from your revenue budget. Use a separate form.

Sub-totals

Sub-totals:

- Set-up costs
- Fixed direct costs
- Variable direct costs
- Indirect costs

are convenient for subsequently calculating unit-costs, and for producing summarised budgets where the mass of detail can be distracting. Where you produce a sub-total in a budget make sure that it is clearly marked by an underlining and a label; you do not want to double count. Make sure that your set-up costs are quite clearly separated from the other, recurrent revenue costs.

It is also common to sub-total all salaries, National Insurance Contribution costs, pension costs and any contingency (for redundancy, sick leave etc) as **"Total salaries"**. This sub-total is often used in formulae for apportioning other costs (e.g. share of premises or management time).

Income

In order to complete your Income and Expenditure Budget you must also work out your assumed income.

- Remember to enter the assumptions you make when calculating a price for a contract.

- If income is not certain, say so.

- If you have shortfall in the budgeted income then show it clearly – either as a "Shortfall" or as "Fundraising Target" or as "Target price" as appropriate.

Warning

The aim of a budget is to project the real expenditure and income of an activity, not to be clever about making the figures balance neatly out.

Figure 8.2a shows a completed Income and Expenditure revenue budget for the cost centre of the Shandy Day Centre, part of the Wadman Widows' Trust.

- For the sake of clarity, the capital expenditure is recorded separately on another sheet and only revenue is shown here.

- It separates set-up costs as distinct from recurring costs eg Telephone connection, as distinct from calls and rental.

- Because they haven't used the premises yet they don't know how much their gas and electricity bills will be. But they make an informed guess.

- The Depreciation Schedule sets out what assets are being depreciated, on what basis and over what term.

- Under indirect costs management and administration is put down as 10% of the central cost centre. Note that Insurance is for the day centre staff and premises only; that of central staff has been included in the central cost centre total.

- Variable costs include not just the food for meals, but also

Figure 8.2a: A COMPLETED I & E BUDGET FOR A COST CENTRE

Wadman Widows' Trust – Income & Expenditure Budget

Cost Centre :	Contract:	Period
02 Shandy Centre	Loamshire B	1993-4

Draft No.2   Date: 2/16.1.93   Prepared by: 1s   Checked: Approved

Cost centre – 02   Year – 1993-4

Revenue Expenditure

Set up Costs		Comments
Research	2,000	Fee to consultant
Recruitment	450	Newspaper advert & interview expenses
Induction	350	Trainers' fees
Legal	150	Lease
Office	250	Minor items
Telephone	180	Connection
Stationery	150	Letterhead
Publicity	300	Design & print launch leaflet
Total Set-up costs	**3,830**	

Direct costs - fixed

Co-ordinator	14,650	Sc. point 27; award of 6% from July 1 '93
Project workers	12,499	2x0.5 @ Sc. point 22, award of 6% from July 1 '93
National Insurance	2,656	Co-ordinator 10.45%, part-timers 9%
Pension	1,357	5% of gross salaries
Staff contingency	779	2.5% total salaries
Total salaries	**31,941**	
Staff training	500	2 residential at £2000 each + 4 speakers @ £25
Staff travel	250	
Rent	1,750	Includes service charge estimated at £250
Rates	0	100% relief (subject to confirmation)
Electricity	250	Guess based on previous tenant's bills + 10%
Gas	350	Heating only – guess as electricity

allowances for the extra gas and (metered) water used over and above the estimate in fixed costs

- Income for the cost centre comes mainly from the contract

Set up Costs		Comments
Water	150	Guess based on previous tenant's bills + 10%
Repair & maintenance	150	
Telephone	500	Rental, calls on one line
Postage	50	
Stationery	75	
Photocopying	50	
Depreciation	1,714	See schedule
Total direct fixed	**37,730**	

Indirect costs		
Management (to 01)	9,016	To central cost centre (01), based on 10% Central staff time
Insurance	350	Employers, contents & public liability Centre staff & premises only
Total indirect costs	**9,366**	
Total fixed costs	**50,926**	
Variable costs		
Catering supplies	3,000	Based on 1500 meals per year
Gas	300	Additional for cooking 1500 meals
Water	30	Additional for cooking 1500 meals
Total variable costs	**3,330**	
Total	**54,256**	Based on assured price + 1500 user/sessions at £2.59 each

Income		
Loamshire B Contract	53,881	
Sales	375	1500 meals at 25 pence each
Total	**54,256**	
BALANCE	0	

with Loamshire, which is priced on a cost and volume basis, with an assured price of £50,000 plus £2.59 for every user/session provided. But the Shandy Centre is also charging users 25p for a meal (part of the session).

Figure 8.2b: A COMPLETED MULT-CENTRE BUDGET						

Wadman Widows' Trust – Income & Expenditure Budget

Cost Centre : All revenue   Contract: All   Period: Apr 93-Mar 94

Draft No.   Date 2/24.1.93   Prepared by: 1s   Checked:

Cost centre:	01 Central	02 Shandy	03 Outreach	04 Spec. Prog	05 Occu-pancy	Total
Expenditure						
Set up costs		3,830				**3,830**
Direct costs - fixed						
Total salaries	77,450	31,941	17,000	23,000	0	**149,391**
Staff training	1,200	500	500	500		**2,700**
Staff travel	750	250	250	250		**1,500**
Occupancy (to 05)	1,500		1,500	1500		**4,500**
Rent		1,750			2,000	**3,750**
Electricity		250			300	**550**
Gas		350			500	**850**
Water		150			200	**350**
Repair & maintenance		150			400	**550**
Telephone	1,750	500	1,000	1,000		**4,250**
Postage	500	50	200	200		**950**
Publicity/printing	800		500	500		**1,800**
Stationery	300	75	100	100		**575**
Photocopying	200	50	100	100		**450**
Library/subscription	500	0	0	0		**500**
Depreciation	1,667	1,714	400	400	1,100	**5,281**
Total direct fixed	**86,617**	**37,730**	**21,550**	**27,550**	**4,500**	**177,947**

Multi-centre budgeting

So far our budget has just concerned one cost centre. If this is all you have, fine, but it is already obvious that we cannot arrive at a final figure for this one cost centre without

Cost centre:	01 Central	02 Shandy	03 Outreach	04 Spec. Prog	05 Occupancy	Total
Indirect costs						
Mgt ctte expenses	250					250
Management (to 01)		9,016	22,539	22,539		54,094
Legal fees	450					450
Insurance	450	350				800
Bank charges	1,800					1,800
Bank interest						0
Audit	590					590
Total indirect costs	**3,540**	**9,366**	**22,539**	**22,539**	**0**	**57,984**
Total fixed costs	**9,0157**	**47,096**	**4,4089**	**50,089**	**4,500**	**235,931**
Total variable costs		**3,330**	**500**	**500**		**4330**
Total expenditure	**90,157**	**50,426**	**44,589**	**50,089**	**4,500**	**240,261**

	01 Central	02 Shandy	03 Outreach	04 Spec. Prog	05 Occupancy	Total
Income						
Contracts		50,051	24,589	45,589		120,229
Grants & donations	32,500		20,000	5,000		57,500
Fees	500					500
Sales		375				375
Subscription	3,063					3,063
Bank interest	0	0	0	0	0	0
Total external	**36,063**	**50,426**	**44,589**	**50,589**	**0**	**181,667**
Internal transfers	**54,094**				**4,500**	**58,594**
Total income	**90,157**	**50,426**	**44,589**	**50,589**	**4,500**	**240,261**
Balance	**0**	**0**	**0**	**0**	**0**	**0**

reviewing some other cost centres. We will also want to fit this partial picture of the organisation's activities into the larger canvas and assess the consequences for the organisation as whole, and for its cash flow. Multi-centre budgeting is the way to produce a stage one "testing feasibility" set of costings comparing going ahead with a contract with not going ahead. It is the only way to be sure that the consequences of changes to one cost-centre are fully worked through the many inter-relationships that may exist. You will need to be sure that you really have provided for 100% of say your HQ administration unit, rather than only 75% .

Figure 8.2b Multi-centre I&E Budget fits the budget for the Shandy Day Centre cost centre (02) into the context of all the cost centres run by the Wadman Widows' Trust. These are 01 Central, 03 Outreach, 04 Special Programme, and 05 Occupancy – a mixture of project/contract and function cost centres.

- Because the Shandy Day Centre occupies its own premises it alone bears the costs of the rent, electricity, gas etc incurred there.

- But Central, Outreach and Special Programme all share an office base, the costs of which are shared through the Occupancy cost centre 05. The apportionment is one-third each, which in fact is considerably out of proportion to the number of staff employed on each. Now it may be that Outreach and Special Programme take up a lot of space (bulky equipment, lots of meetings with large numbers of users). Or the person who drew up this budget is overcharging better-funded contract or grant-aided cost centres in order to cross-subsidise the under-funded central cost centre. And they are doing it without increasing the indirect costs of management.

- The payments that the Shandy Centre, Outreach and Special programme make to central for Management appear under each of those cost centres in the class of expenditure "Management".

- Payments between cost centres do not constitute real additional income, and so appear, totalled separately, under the class of Income "Internal transfers" under the appropriate cost centres.

- Set Up, Total Salary and Variable Costs are consolidated.

- The right-hand column totals classes of Expenditure for the whole organisation. This is the basis for calculating cash-flow. These totals are used for distributing total expenditure month-by-month across the year.

- Because cash-flow has not yet been calculated both the Expenditure Bank Interest row (cost of borrowing) and the Income Bank Interest row (return on invested surpluses) are both blank. When they are filled in the policy of the Wadman Widows trustees is to set interest solely against the Central cost centre, and so shared as part of the general apportionment of indirect costs between the other cost centres.

Taking care

There is nothing intrinsically difficult about multi-centre budgeting. However with several cost centres the number of calculations to be performed quickly escalates; the paper grows unwieldy, and errors occur more frequently.

Using a spreadsheet undoubtedly will speed up the calculations, but it still takes time to move around a large spreadsheet and great care must still be taken particularly in copying formulae (see Appendix 1 Checking and Appendix 2 Using Computers).

Multi-year forecasting

It is prudent to look more than one year ahead in budgeting. But the further ahead you look the harder it obviously becomes to give detailed accurate estimates. Concentrate instead on identifying the factors which will change the basis of your costing, and making broad allowances for them. These might include an increase in the volume or change in the nature of a service or passing a break point (see Chapter 11). Remember to allow for progressive increases not due to inflation like staff wage increments.

Figure 8.3: MULTI-YEAR BUDGET

Wadma Widows' Trust – Income & Expenditure Budget

Cost Centre : 02 Shady Centre					Contract: Loamshire B Period 1993-4
Draft No.2 Date: 2/16.1.93	Prepared by: 1s		Checked:		Approved
Year	1993-4	1994-5	1995-6	TOTAL	**Comments**
					No allowance for inflation after 1993-4
Revenue Expenditure					
Set up costs	3,830		1,000	4,830	See Schedules 3 and 4
Direct costs - fixed					
Co-ordinator	14,650	15,136	15,136	44,922	Starts at Sc. point 27, award of 6% from July 1 1993. Reaches top of scale
Project workers	12,499	12,872	13,299	38,670	2 X 0.5 starting at Sc. point 22; award of 6% from July 1 1993
Education workers	0	0	12,499	12,499	Starting at Sc. point 22 1 April 1995
National Insurance	2,656	2,740	4,085	9,481	Full-timers 10.45%, part-timers 9%
Pension	1,357	1,400	2,047	4,805	5% of gross salaries
Staff contingency	779	804	1,177	2,759	2.5% total salaries
Total salaries	**31,941**	**32,952**	**48,242**	**113,136**	
Staff training	500	500	750	1,750	2 residential courses at £200 each + 4 speakers @ £25 each year
Staff travel	250	250	350	850	Mainly coordinator to & fro HQ. Education worker in Year 3.
Rent	1,750	2,125	2,500	6,375	Includes service charge. Rent review from 1 Sept 1994
Rates	0	0	0	0	100% relief (subject to confirmation)
Electricity	250	250	300	800	Guess based on previous tenant's bills + 10%
Gas	350	350	350	1,050	Heating only – guess based on previous tenant's bills + 10%
Water	150	150	150	450	Guess based on previous tenant's bills + 10%
Repair & maintenance	150	250	250	650	Redecoration by 31 Aug 1994, increasing wear & tear
Telephone	500	500	600	1,600	1 line. 1995-6 additional use by education worker
Postage	50	50	60	160	1995-6 additional use by education worker
Stationery	75	75	100	250	1995-6 additional use by education worker
Photocopying	50	50	100	200	1995-6 additional use by education worker
Depreciation	1,714	1,714	2,114	5,542	See schedule 5
Total direct fixed	**37,730**	**39,216**	**55,866**	**132,813**	

Indirect costs

Year	1993-4	1994-5	1995-6	TOTAL	Comments
Indirect costs					
Management & Admin	9,016	9,016	13,524	31,556	To central cost centre, 10% Central staff time, 15% in 1995-????
Insurance	350	350	450	1,150	Employers, contents & public liability Centre staff & premises only
Total indirect costs	9,366	9,366	13,974	32,706	
Total fixed costs	**50,926**	**48,582**	**70,840**	**170,349**	

Year	1993-4	1994-5	1995-6	TOTAL	Comments
Variable costs					
Catering supplies	3,000	4,000	5,000	12,000	Meal no's per year rising from 1500 through 2000 to 2500
Gas	300	400	500	1,200	Additional for cooking meals
Water	30	40	50	120	Additional for cooking meals
Consumables		0	500	500	Education materials
Total variable costs	**3,330**	**4,440**	**6,050**	**13,820**	
TOTAL REVENUE EXPENDITURES	**54,256**	**53,022**	**76,890**	**184,169**	

Year	1993-4	1994-5	1995-6	TOTAL	Comments
Income					
Loamshire B Contract	53,881	55,180	56,475	165,536	Assured grant £50,000 + £2.59 per user session
Sales	375	500	625	1,500	Meals @ 25p each
Grant			17,133	17,133	Target for grant applications
Brought forward		0	2,657		
Total Income	**54,256**	**55,680**	**74,233**	**184,169**	
Balance	0	2,657	0		

Allow a margin for error and contingency. You may find it easier to consolidate classes of expenditure and income.

Make sure you include full notes on what assumptions the projection is based on.

Figure 8.3 shows a three year projection for one cost centre, the Shandy centre.

- Over the three years it is hoped that the Centre will increase the number of user/sessions from 1,500 to 2000 and 2,500 in the second and third years.

- It is planned to take on a full-time education worker in the third year.

- That post will incur some capital expenditure; some set-up costs, some marginal additional Direct costs and Variable Costs. Indirect Costs are projected to rise by 50% in proportion with the increase in staff numbers.

- Schedule 1 gives full details of the capital purchases to be made in 1993-94; schedule 2 gives details for a second phase of capital expenditure in 1995-96. Schedules 3 and 4 do the same for set-up costs.

- Under Income is a "Brought Forward" row so that surplus or deficit incurred in one year goes into the next year's calculations. So there is a surplus at the end of 1994-95 of £2,657 which contributes to the income of 1995-96.

- However that surplus is not enough to meet all the costs associated with the new education worker, and the shortfall is shown as a target for grant applications, thus balancing the budget.

Multi-centre, multi-year forecasts

From projections like this for all the other cost centres you can draw up a three or five year forecast for your whole organisation. Obviously, in a strategic planning exercise you must sacrifice detail in order to be able to see the whole picture. But you should retain enough detail in order to be able to distinguish the performance of individual cost centres. It can be difficult to show with any clarity say four or five cost centres projected over three years. For most purposes it is more helpful to prepare:

- three separate sheets, each one showing the projection for one of three successive years for all the cost centres together, and

- a summary sheet showing whole organisation totals for three years.

Predicting inflation

Multi-year budgets should state clearly whether any allowance has been made for inflation, and if so on what basis.

There are advantages in preparing an multi-year budget in which no allowance has been made for inflation, particularly during a period of expansion. You are able to compare so-called "real" costs without the complication of compounding inflation. You may then be able to detect costs escalating for other reasons or identify economies arising from a larger scale of operation. It may also be easier to then revise any subsequent calculation of the effects of inflation.

However when it comes to pricing a contract you must include a carefully considered allowance for inflation in your calculations. You must be sure that the costs you have supplied for year 1 are at the prices you will have to pay then, not at this year's prices. And unless there is a clear explicit commitment to index-linking in the terms of the contract you should examine each line of your expenditure budget and correct it for inflation in subsequent years as seems most appropriate. Beware of adding a fixed percentage to the total.

If the contract pricing system is geared in whole or part to the rate of inflation check that the mechanism used and the index used is appropriate to the actual costs you will be incurring.

If the rate of inflation is rising rapidly you need to ensure that price reviews happen frequently enough to safeguard your cash-flow.

Are there any claw-back clauses whereby the purchaser recovers money already paid to you if the rate of inflation falls?

Inflation makes money worth less, and so raises prices. But it does not operate uniformly across the economy. Property prices may rise more quickly than say the prices of manufactured goods. Look behind the headline figure which is based on the Retail Price Index (RPI) – in effect a household shopping basket. Voluntary organisations should pay particular attention to wage settlements in the public sector, because staff costs tend to bulk so large in social care budgets that even a small percentage discrepancy can produce large real shortfalls.

If petrol – or motor transport – is a large item in your budget you should be aware that the price of this commodity is subject to sudden and large increases. Can you afford to assume that there will not be another war or crisis in the Gulf or Middle East?

Other longer-term considerations

• Staff movements & other contingencies.
While it may be difficult to cost for the kinds of staff contingencies discussed in Section 2 in short-term budgets, it is imperative to do so in longer term projections. More unlikely things are likely to happen over longer periods of time.

• Repairs
Bear in mind that ageing assets (equipment, vehicles, premises) – require more maintenance and more frequent and expensive repair.

• Renewals
Some assets may need to be replaced. Even if they have been

fully depreciated- and the depreciation fund is still intact – changes in design or requirements may mean additional costs to effect replacements.

• Leases

The renewal or mid term review of leases can produce some dramatic increases in rents, particularly if the lease has been held for a long time. Some leases on premises specify redecoration at the end of the lease.

Morag >> *a continuing story* (from Page 105)

Morag considered if she should extend her costing into further years, as Dr. Anderson had said that most of the Health Centre's programmes were based on a three year commitment. But this seemed impossible for such a small and possibly short-lived project, so she left it.

(Continued on Page 139)

Chapter 9
Predicting Cash Flow

The Income and Expenditure Budget tells us how much money we think we will receive and spend over a whole year; Cash Flow forecasts tell us how much money we need at a given moment in time to meet all the expenditure due.

This chapter will show you how to forecast your organisation's cash flow and how to calculate the amount of working capital needed. We need to work out the cash flow in order to ensure that we have enough money in hand to spend when it is needed. This is done by looking at each month and totalling the money you expect to receive and the money you expect to spend in each month. A cumulating balance – either a surplus (more income than expenditure) or deficit (more expenditure than income) is then carried forward to add to the next months calculation. Deficits – which are negative amounts or losses – are shown in brackets.

Figure 9.1 shows a simple Cash Flow forecast. It assumes that there are no deficits or surpluses to carry forward into April from the previous year. Income for the month exceeds total expenditure by £1,900; a surplus that is carried forward to May. In May, however, in spite of that boost, expenditure exceeds income, producing a deficit of £745, carried forward to June, and so on through the year.

Note that the Cumulating Balance fluctuates between surplus and deficit from month to month in spite of the fact that over the year Total Income and Total Expenditure are budgeted to balance. Note also that totalling balances is meaningless.

Remember that cash flow is about when money enters or leaves your organisation or its bank accounts. Internal transactions between cost centres do not count.

Cash flow – expenditure: important considerations

In plotting cash flow you need to think carefully about the practical working of your operation.

Look first at Expenditure: Are there any seasonal variations? Do you take on extra volunteers, say over the summer? Should you look for higher levels of expenses payments in August and September? What about fluctuations in fuel bills?

Do you need to hold stocks of any kind? You may be providing meals to your users. How many days' supplies of food will you hold in hand? What about bulk purchases of staples? How are creditors to be paid – on receipt of invoice, or through a monthly account?

You will know that you must pay electricity, gas, phone bills at every quarter. Unless you have definite indications to the contrary assume the worst and make the first payments fall due in the first month.

What assumptions are you making about the use of your service? Say your costings are based on providing a service to 30 users, in three consecutive groups of 10, each of which bring an allowance of £100. What if you cannot fill all 30 places? What if 25 want to start in April and only 5 in September and January?

What about the payment of capital expenditure? What about any delays in the delivery, installation and full operation of plant and equipment, without which income cannot be earned from users?

Remember that when the volume of services is increasing your outgoings are likely to rise immediately; you take on more staff, have to buy more food for the daily lunch, make

Figure 9.1: CASH FLOW FORECAST

	Income	Less expenditure	Plus carried forward	Cumulating balance
April	5,500	3,500		1,900
May	300	2,985	1,900	(745)
June	500	3,000	(745)	(3,245)
July	7,500	2,875	(3,245)	1,380
Year Totals	40,420	40,420	0	

more journeys in the van. Your income, however, is likely to rise later. A gap of only a couple of months could be quite significant.

Cash flow – P.A.Y.E. and VAT

The employees' Income Tax and National Insurance payments collected through PAYE (and the employers' National Insurance Contribution) must be paid by the 19th of the month after the wages were paid. So if you employ several staff this delay could have a considerable (favourable) impact on your cash flow. It may be worth showing the net wages and deductions as two separate classes of expenditure and including the corresponding amount of the latter in your total of expenditure one month after the former (but it may not; you must decide). Don't forget that you will have to start the projection for the next period by carrying forward the deduction for the last month of the preceding year.

VAT and cash flow

At the end of each three-month VAT period you have to complete a VAT return stating the total output tax you have charged and the total input tax you have billed for. You deduct the value of the input tax from the output tax and send the difference to HM Customs and Excise. This is due one month after the end of the VAT period.

If your input tax during the period was greater than the output tax then you will get a refund from the VAT office.

For organisations with a turnover of less than £300,000 per year there is a special cash accounting scheme which lets you base your VAT payments on the actual output tax you have received and input tax you have paid during the period, instead of basing it on what you have charged (but perhaps not yet received) and what you have been billed for (but perhaps not yet paid).

On your cashflow projection the input tax must be included in the period when you expect to pay your suppliers, and output tax should be included when payments from customers are expected. You must also add in the net payment to Customs and Excise at the point where your return is due.

Cash flow – Income: important considerations

On the income side you need again to take a pessimistic view of the speed with which payments will be made to you by others. There may in any case be an inbuilt delay between you providing a service incurring a cost, and banking the income due to cover it.

Pay particular attention to your own invoicing and debt collection procedures. If you get income through issuing large numbers of invoices you will need a system to monitor the amount of money owed to you, like preparing a weekly or monthly list of debts, ranked by age.

Be particularly wary of third party agreements where you send your invoice to the recipient of the service who must then either obtain authorisation from someone else, or pass it to someone else for payment.

Calculating your working capital

We can assess our need for Working Capital by looking at the size and distribution of the monthly cash flow deficits. It is not enough to read off the largest deficit, however.

A month is the conventional accounting period for cash-flow calculations and will suit the purposes of most voluntary groups. However if you think that you will be receiving and paying out exceptionally large sums of money within a period of less than a month then you should undertake a more detailed study based on a daily analysis of that period.

Figure 9.2 shows a Cash Flow Forecast for the Careless Trust. Payments for the contract are made quarterly in arrears. Look carefully to see what the Working Capital requirement actually is. Suppose payment of the first instalment of £11,000 is due on the 30th June. But the Trust pays staff their wages on the 26th of the month. So though the cash flow suggests that their maximum capital requirement is £9,000, there may be a time near the end of every third month when they need £11,000 to £12,000, depending on the size of the wage bill.

CASH-FLOW WITH CARE

Before we look at where this working capital is to come from, it is worth reflecting on one of the Golden Rules of Guessing

Things will take longer than you think;

Unforeseen delays will always outweigh unforeseen savings of time.

This is almost certain to be the case in the signing of contracts.

What are the consequences for your cash flow if the start date of your budget is put back one – or three – or six months?

Sources of working capital

Where can working capital come from?

There are three possible sources:

Pay creditors later

High interest rates and sophisticated computerised accounting techniques have made late payment of bills a common practice for many large companies, to the despair of most smaller enterprises. For many smaller voluntary organisations the principal items of expenditure are staff salaries. These simply have to be paid on time.

	Income	Less expenditure	Plus carried forward	Cumulating balance
Figure 9.2: CARELESS TRUST CASH FLOW FORECAST – income paid quarterly in arrears				
April	0	5,500		(5,500)
May	0	3,500	(5,500)	(9,000)
June	11,000	3,500	(9,000)	(1,500)
July	0	3,500	(1,500)	(5,000)
Aug		3,500	(5,000)	(8,500)
Sep	11,000	3,500	(8,500)	(1,000)
Oct		3,500	(1,000)	(4,500)
Nov		3,500	(4,500)	(8,000)
Dec	11,000	3,500	(8,000)	(500)
Jan		3,500	(500)	(4,000)
Feb		3,500	(4,000)	(7,500)
Mar	11,000	3,500	(7,500)	0
Year total	**44,000**	**44,000**	**0**	**0**

Get debtors to pay more earlier

Getting debtors to pay earlier is an option to consider in the negotiation of a contract: payment in advance rather than arrears, at half-yearly rather than quarterly or even monthly intervals; these kinds of financial arrangements can make a substantial difference to the value of a contract.

Figure 9.3 shows the cash flow of the Careless Trust if the contract payments were made quarterly in advance (expenditure pattern being the same). Interest paid by a bank on the 9 months of surpluses (some quite substantial) would probably at least cancel out interest paid to the bank on overdrafts to cover the 3 months of (relatively small) deficits. In Figure 9.2 you can see that payment quarterly in arrears means that there is a cash deficit to be financed in every month apart from the last.

Borrow money from somewhere else to bridge the gap

There are four possible sources. The first two are likely to prove considerably cheaper to voluntary organisations.

Use the organisation's own reserves

It is usually cheaper – in terms of the effective rate of interest – to lend yourself your own money. Interest charges on the sum borrowed from a bank will usually outweigh the interest payments on the same sum lent to a bank. You cannot divert funds donated to your organisation for specific charitable purposes to other, or non-charitable activities. Take advice from NCVO or the Charity Commission if in doubt. You must also make a prudent assessment of the possible calls on your organisation's reserves from other areas of activity. Of course your organisation may not have any cash reserves.

If your organisation as a whole is effectively "floating" the contract operation then you should know what that is costing your organisation – i.e. the lost interest payments on the capital sum required, plus any increased interest charges incurred through the loss of available cash to finance other areas of your organisation's work. These are costs which you may wish to negotiate into the contract price.

Borrow from the purchaser of your services

Financing the cash flow is a legitimate cost of providing the service which it will be in the purchaser's interest to ensure is done as economically as possible. In many cases this will

	Income	Less expenditure	Plus carried forward	Cumulating balance
Figure 9.3 : CARELESS TRUST CASH FLOW FORECAST – income paid quarterly in advance				
April	11,000	5,500		5,500
May	0	3,500	5,500	2,000
June		3,500	2,000	(1,500)
July	11,000	3,500	(1,500)	6,000
Aug		3,500	6,000	2,500
Sep		3,500	2,500	(1,000)
Oct	11,000	3,500	(1,000)	6,500
Nov		3,500	6,500	3,000
Dec		3,500	3,000	(500)
Jan	11,000	3,500	(500)	7,000
Feb		3,500	7,000	3,500
Mar		3,500	3,500	0
Year total	**44,000**	**44,000**	**0**	**0**

be achieved through negotiating a payment schedule matched to the demands of the cash-flow budget. This is a form of getting a debtor to pay up earlier. Or the purchaser may make a "soft" loan at lower than commercial interest rates. This may be attractive to some purchasers wishing to contribute to some capital investment required for a contract.

In some contracts, however, the purchaser of the contract service may also be a supplier (of stock or services through, for example, the local authority purchasing organisation), or creditor (for example as landlord) to the provider of the contract service. Under these circumstances you will be well advised to review all of your financial relationships with the purchaser. You may wish to try to negotiate a peppercorn rent (thereby reducing your expenditure) instead of looking for a loan. This kind of arrangement could be of great benefit to your organisation if for example you thereby reduce the overheads of other, non-contract activities based on the premises. Taking such a global view of the financial relationships between purchaser and provider may be beyond the competence of care budget managers, and any proposals you may make will certainly be more easily realised if they have support from say, a relevant committee chair, or even the Policy Unit or Leader of the Council.

Two elements of the A.M.A.'s guidance to local authorities should be borne in mind at this point

"It is important to ensure that contracts are not negotiated in isolation from the SSD's financial officers".

"Those involved with financial arrangements within any local authority, including elected members, must be aware of the relationship between the budgetary cycle and the honouring of contracts. Local authorities must be committed to ensuring payments for services on time"

We are at present in the early stages of contracts, when local authority officers and members have little experience of incorporating the requirements of contract commitments into their financial decision-making processes. Those processes are in turn under great pressure from the debacle of the poll tax and central government intervention in local authority finance. Voluntary organisations entering into contracts would be prudent to (a) press for explicit penalties in the contract to recompense them for defaults on the payment schedule and (b) plan for the contingency of payments not being made on time.

Borrowing money is not be undertaken lightly. If you are a trust you will need to ensure that your articles of association give officers the powers to borrow money. You should take advice from your accountant, and if need be, the Charity Commission. Incurring costs you could avoid may be seen as a breach of trust.

Borrowing on the commercial money market

Banks and other financial institutions may lend you the money subject to you producing a convincing business plan. This is likely to be a relatively expensive option. British banks have an appalling record for milking small and medium sized enterprises through their lending practices.

Borrowing from your creditors

The people to whom you must pay money – are another source of credit. If you are purchasing substantial values of supplies you may be able to negotiate credit – approved delayed payment in other words – but at a price. This may be undertaken in conjunction with a third party finance house, and would probably prove the most expensive option of all.

You must also consider your monthly cash surpluses, and what action you will take to make the best – but prudent – use of these. The BCCI collapse lost the short term cash surpluses of many local authorities. If you have some short-term surpluses to invest then:

- Shop around,
- Take advice,
- Spread the risk,
- Don't be greedy for that extra half percent,
- Don't tell the purchasing authority unless you're sure they won't claw it back.

If you decide that you need to borrow money you will incur additional expenditure in the form of interest charges. You may also incur higher levels of bank charges on all your transactions if you run your bank account into the red. You will need to investigate this possibility with your bank as practices vary greatly and many banks are changing their charging structures.

You must now work the costs of supplying your working capital back into your I & E budget. If these are substantial you will then have to revise your cash flow forecast and I&E budget again and again until you reach a point where the discrepancies are no more than 10% (for a preliminary budgeting exercise) or 5% (for pricing purposes).

Morag >> *a continuing story* (from Page 128)

Morag was very aware of the importance of her cash flow. Two years earlier she had found herself unable to write cheques for the expenses of a group of volunteers because a grant she had been promised by the Southtown Parish Charities had not come in (because the Treasurer was in hospital). The Project's constitution did not allow it to run an overdraft and she had had to lend the money herself (and even this was still unconstitutional!)

She now totalled up the costs of the new project for the year and divided them up into twelve equal monthly amounts, less the £100 for the filing cabinet and the £200 for contract preparation time, all of which she put in month 1. She knew that many of her bills came in arrears, so this arrangement was cautious. It worked out that she needed £675 at the beginning of each month plus an extra amount of £300 at the beginning of the new project.

(Continued on Page 143)

Chapter 10

Formulating and calculating Unit Costs

What are Unit Costs?

Unit Costs are the Total Costs of a service divided by the number of Units of provision. So as well as calculating the costs you have to define what the Unit of provision (or Unit of service) is. It must be something that can be expressed as a number, or as a formula which will produce a number (number of user visits; number of trainees x number of hours of training each receives).

Where the volume of service cannot be known in advance the purchaser may wish to specify pricing by unit costs in order to guarantee value for money. Then they only pay for units of provision actually delivered.

Take care in selecting measures for the output of your work. Lumping together different kinds of clients – or different kinds of activities can produce meaningless averages.

Unit Costs – an example

An Advice Centre's total costs are £100,000 a year. They deal with 500 clients in that time. Therefore the Unit Cost per client would appear to be £200.

But 100 clients were serious cases requiring more than 3 hours work per client. Taken together those 100 clients occupied 75% of the centre's resources of staff time etc.

So the Unit Cost per serious case client is 75% x £100,000 / 100 = £750.

And the Unit Cost per other clients would be 25% x £100,000/ 400 = £62.50

But in fact you don't get 100 serious case clients without seeing many others. After all you can't just take the first 100 clients in through the door and turn them into serious cases. A thorough understanding of your organisation's break points (see Chapter 11) and consultation with those who actually provide the service should help to avoid these kinds of pitfalls. They are essential to drawing up a realistic picture of serious case and other clients in our example. You may find that instead of using numbers of clients as units that it is better to use hours of advice given: it's a more flexible measure, and better reflects the difficulties associated with serious cases.

Comparisons between Unit Costs from different organisations should be treated with especial caution. Enormous discrepancies can occur depending on the what is included – and what is omitted from – indirect costs. This is particular danger where a purchaser has provided a similar service in-house in the past. In order to compare like with like you have to be sure that the methods of calculation are the same, and that the service provided is to the same standard.

COMPARING UNIT COSTS

Some factors influencing total costs

| Indirect Costs | Pay scales |
| Inflation assumptions | Depreciation fund |

Some factors affecting the number of units:

Non-productive staff time (holidays, sickness, administration etc)

Frequency of service	Sequence of activities
Peaks and troughs in demand	Waiting lists
Third party delays	Vacancy Rates

At this point Dr Anderson rang Morag to say she had better get on with it, as budget decisions were beginning to be taken; and incidentally, could she also express her figures, when she had them ready, as a cost per child?

This latter looked easy. Morag took the total budget and divided it by 60, the number of children proposed, giving a figure of £135 a child. She also worked it out as a cost per club of ten children, at £1,350 per club.

Munster Project – Costs

	Main Project	New Project	**TOTAL**
Salary (P/T Co-ordinator and P/T Assistant)	£9,000	£4,500	**13,500**
Premises/office costs (donated by SS)	£2,000	£1,000	**3,000**
Administration costs	£825	£412	**1,237**
Club and volunteer costs	£2,380	£1,190	**3,570**
Evaluation		£1,000	**1,000**
	14,205	**8,102**	**22,307**

One-off cost: Filing cabinet at	£100
Contract preparation at £10/hr	£200
	£300

(Continued on Page 153)

143

PART 4

PUTTING COSTING INTO PRACTICE IN THREE STAGES

Chapter 11
Deciding to take on a contract or not

The first stage in costing is to use the information to decide whether or not to pursue – or accept – a contract. You need to establish the conditions under which taking on a given contract is viable and acceptable.

Your first aim will be to see if the actual costs of providing the specified service are within negotiating distance of the amount of money on offer.

You will then be looking to be compare the effects on your organisation of going ahead with a contract with the effects of not going ahead.

What new costs would a contract bring?

If taking on a contract will mean an expansion or change in your services you will need to assess how much more you need to spend to meet the requirements of the contract.

You need to analyse the resources your organisation commands and how they are deployed – sometimes referred to as the cost structure. You will be looking to see what level/volume of service can be supported by current unused capacity without making the break to the next level of expenditure.

Look for the critical break points in how your organisation deploys its resources, that is, the points at which costs will jump sharply. What is the present unused capacity? – what level of service could it support? And once that is used up, what do you step up to – what then becomes your unused capacity – and what happens to your overheads?

FIGURE 11.1: BREAK POINTS

An advice worker must be paid, trained, managed and maintained in an office and interview room; publicity to tell the world she is there must be produced, and she must subscribe to information update services and so on, regardless of how many clients she sees in a week. There will be a limit, however, to the number of people that she can see. In a text-book world we might say that the upper limit is 60 people per week; and that in order to serve the 61st and 62nd clients you must employ a second worker. Let us look at what that might cost.

Total Salary Costs1 worker salary & NIC	15,000
Overheads	5,000
	20,000

60 clients x 47 weeks = 2,820 clients therefore unit cost per client = 20,000/2820 = £7.09

2 workers salaries & NIC	30,000
Overheads	5,000
	35,000

62 clients x 47 weeks = 2,914 clients
Therefore, unit cost per client = 35,000/2,914 = £12.01
Obviously increasing the number of clients seen by the second worker would reduce the unit cost.

But of course the real world is not like this. 60 clients do not present themselves at half-hourly intervals throughout the week. Even with an appointment system, some interviews will over-run, or require exceptional follow-up work, and many clients will be unable to attend except at "peak" times.

In the voluntary sector break points are rarely sharply marked points at all; they are grey areas. The very flexibility of the voluntary sector stems in part from its capacity to stretch its break points, through the ingenuity and commitment of its staff and volunteers. However though voluntary organisations have elastic capacities, they are finite. If you operate indefinitely in the grey area (perhaps we should say red zone) of stretched capacity then sooner or later something will give: staff, volunteers, quality or other areas of work.

Key break points

You may need to make yourself familiar with how and when the following key break points occur in your organisation:

- Service delivery staff
- Support and supervisory staff
- Administration and management staff
- Premises
- Vehicles
- Other equipment
- Cash flow

You will be making this analysis bearing in mind the following factors:

- The recruitment and training of new staff. Is your ability to carry out the service dependent on the skills and experience built up by your existing staff? How will you replace them if they leave?
- Due allowance for the higher cost of maintenance repair and proper depreciation of all the assets employed – vehicles, equipment, fixtures and fittings.
- A fair contribution to management and administrative costs

- The cost of negotiating the contract.
- The cost of establishing and maintaining quality assurance and quality monitoring systems required in the contract.
- The cost of establishing any new accounting systems.
- How capital purchases are to be financed.
- The consequences for your organisation's cash flow of e.g. purchasing stocks.
- The consequences of VAT registration (if this is necessary).

The steps you need to take

You should prepare an Income and Expenditure Budget for a new cost centre for the contract service, as described in Chapter 8. If the service is a substantial part of your organisation's activities, or is likely to have many "trading links" with other cost centres then you should re-work the entire I&E Budgets for the whole organisation.

You will in any case need to look at the rest of your I&E budgets to work out the impact of the contract service on your Cash Flow. As we saw in Chapter 9, the cash flow of one cost centre cannot be considered in isolation from the cash flow of the whole organisation.

You should also make some projections into future years – at least 3 years to see what the longer term implications of taking on a particular contract might be.

You may find it easier to consolidate classes of expenditure (see Chapter 2). But just because this is a preliminary costing that doesn't mean you can leave costs out. It may be difficult at this stage to give exact figures – the contract specification may well not be fully worked out. See Box **"Dealing with Approximate Figures"**. You would be well advised to build in at this stage a sizeable safety margin for contingencies.

DEALING WITH APPROXIMATE FIGURES

You may not be able to pin down all the costs of the service in detail, though you will want to survey all the categories of costs to be incurred.

In the early stages of costing it can be helpful to give a minimum/maximum range rather than a precise figure.

For example, the operation of the contract service will require new office premises. You know you will need approximately 2,000 square feet, but you haven't yet found the right place, and so have no figure you can put down for rent. But a couple of phone calls to your local council Economic Development Unit and commercial letting estate agents will tell you the range of rentals for city centre office accommodation. You discover that the cheapest is going for £4.50 per square foot (poor quality, bad access) and that prestige newly refurbished suites start at £15.00 per square foot. You may guess from this that you will need to pay at least £6.00 to get your minimum requirements; but there should be no need to pay more than £15.00. So instead of drawing up a single column of figures you draw up two – showing the minimum and maximum limits of the ranges thus:

Figure 11.2	Minimum	Maximum
Total salary costs	35,000	40,000
Other running costs	10,000	13,000
Rent 2,000 sq ft	12,000	30,000
Other overheads	8,000	12,000
Totals	**65,000**	**95,000**

Minimum and maximum values can then be totalled. This approach is recommended when there are many uncertainties about the how the contract service is to be delivered. It is often better to say "We believe that the service will cost between £65,000 and £95,000 a year" rather than quote a mid figure (in this case £80,000), which may, through use, start to acquire a credibility it does not deserve.

To contract or not to contract?

You should be thinking strategically about the requirements of the contract in the context of other services you may wish to maintain and/or developments you may want to bring about. You need to look beyond the process of getting the contract and the first year's work. How do the consequences compare in 3 year or 5 or 10 years time?

If the prospective contract is likely to form a substantial part of your organisation's activities then you should also draw up Income and Expenditure budgets projected for 3 years and cash flow forecasts for the whole organisation based on not going ahead with a contract.

You would then be in a position to make a comparison.

The point of this comparative exercise is to focus your attention – and that of your colleagues – on two aspects of what may be described as "Opportunity Costs".

Earmarking resources

There are very practical considerations regarding how you earmark resources for future use. Look at your break points. By taking on a contract you may be using resources which at present are under-employed. But by doing so you may be robbing another area of activity of its capacity for growth. A typical example would be empty office space within your premises. The contract service could occupy those for its management and administration at marginal extra expense – fine. But they may leave another activity, which is already in existence and doing well and likely to want more space in the not-too-distant future – with nowhere to expand into. Who then bears the considerable extra cost of making the break to leasing other premises?

You should also consider your organisation's reserves. If taking on a contract means expansion do you have the necessary reserves to back the higher level of financial commitments, either as working capital or as contingency?

Only by looking at all the organisation's activities, and comparing Income and Expenditure over the mid to long term can such hidden costs be uncovered.

Non-renewable sources of human energy

This too concerns the allocation of resources. Some of these cannot be renewed or increased, at any price. Not even voluntary organisations have infinite reserves of initiative, or staff and volunteer time. Taking on a contract may, ipso facto, diminish the capacity of an organisation to maintain or develop existing services, or mount other new initiatives. Drawing up a costing of all the organisations development plans should make you think through who is actually going to do all the development and management and administrative work. If you reach your ceiling, how will that affect your ability to continue to maintain the quality of other, non-contract services, or maintain other, non-contract sources of income?

Deciding to take on a care contract or not can obviously never be done on cost criteria alone. Nor can such a decision be taken without reference to the cost implications for the whole organisation, as this chapter has shown.

If you decide to enter into serious discussions with a prospective contract purchaser you should keep that perspective firmly in mind. But read the next chapter first.

Morag >> *a continuing story* (from Page 143)

Morag was now ready to consult her Management Committee. She took them through the figures; it took a long time, but eventually everyone seemed to have a fair grasp of what they represented. The committee agreed to accept them as a basis on which she could now go back to Dr Anderson.

(Continued on Page 167)

Chapter 12

Pricing and negotiation

So far in this book we have been looking at the costs of providing a service to the organisation providing it. In this section we will be looking at how to turn those into a price that the provider can charge the purchasing organisation; and at the value of costing information in subsequent negotiations. But sometimes a purchasing authority will impose a contract with a non-negotiable price. So we will also look at how to calculate a level of service for a given price.

Sizing up the purchaser

Before deciding on a pricing strategy and before beginning negotiation, it is important to make some analysis of the relationship between the two parties: the purchasing and providing organisations. It is usually very easy to tell who has the most power. What is of more interest is to isolate the purchaser's desires and your capacity to meet them, and their weaknesses and your capacity to exploit them.

The extent to which each party occupies a monopoly position will be an important factor.

Maximum advantage accrues to the purchaser where the provider has no alternative source of income, and the purchaser has a choice of providers.

Maximum advantage to the provider comes where the provider is supplying a range of other purchasers and there is no alternative provider the purchaser can get the service from.

Obviously a number of intermediate conditions can obtain. You need to make your assessment of where to place your relationship with purchasing authorities between these two limits.

But there is a "mixed economy of care". Though being called on to trade in a market place, neither purchasers nor providers are free agents as market traders. Their competitiveness is bound by the nature of the services they are buying and selling and by their nature as public service organisations.

NOT A LEVEL PLAYING FIELD

Another organisation may be able to undercut your price and still offer same quality on the same assumptions. How?
There are many possible reasons. They may, for example,

- Have hidden subsidies from core funding of central costs from central government or elsewhere;
- Happen to have bought what turns out to be the right very large building x years ago;
- Be larger anyway to begin with – fewer break points crossed and more unused capacity.
- Engage in deliberate loss-leading
- Have got their sums wrong.

How the purchaser views pricing

If you are negotiating a contract it is useful to know how the purchaser understands pricing. It is like looking at their cards – or some of them at least.

The Social Services Inspectorate in its guidance "Purchase of Service" distinguishes three kinds of pricing formulae, and provides a useful summary of the pros and cons of each for both purchaser and provider. This is the advice Social Service Departments ("SSDs") will all have received, and I am grateful to the SSI for their kind permission to reproduce the following extract.

Block contracts

These are contracts purchasing access to facilities rather than services for a defined number of clients. Block contracts specify the quantity and quality of inputs rather than outputs.

- Since SSDs would not be paying by volume or by case they would have an incentive to maximise the use and complexity of the service under contract. However, the provider would be expected to take this into account in annual price negotiation.

- Providers have a guaranteed income but face uncertainty over volume and case complexity. They therefore have the incentive to limit their costs whilst fulfilling their contractual obligations.

- SSDs may negotiate block contracts with one or a small number of providers. This will limit consumer choice and will also mean that some providers may be forced out of the market.

Price by case contracts

In these contracts the price is quoted for each type of case or unit of provision and the services are purchased as required. Some SSDs have compiled lists of accredited suppliers from whom such purchases can be made.

- If prices are sufficiently low, then SSDs will be encouraged to purchase a quantity of services. Providers will try to operate at the volume that maximises their profits at expected prices and costs. They may try to control costs by limiting the service they provide to clients and increase revenue by stressing the complexity of each case.

- Providers are uncertain of the number of clients they will receive and may have to make provision for clients who never in fact arrive. SSDs will be financially at risk if they cannot monitor providers sufficiently to prevent case complexity and price being overstated.

- Price by case contracts are flexible and potentially provide a high degree of consumer choice. However, some providers may be unwilling to continue service provision without some form of guaranteed income. Price by case contracts are specific to each type of case or unit of provision, so can be drawn up in considerable detail. As a result the transaction costs of negotiating the price of such contracts can be high.

- One form of price by case contract is the "spot" contract. They are single individual transactions unrelated to any other arrangement. They are usually made in a market with many buyers and suppliers. The cost of the service is agreed at the time of the transaction.

- SSDs may also negotiate a contract which stipulates that the provider will supply services as and when required and at a predetermined fixed price per case. SSDs then take or "call off" services as necessary. This places all the risk with the provider.

Cost and volume contracts

These contracts specify a volume of service and a total cost. A quantity of service is purchased for an agreed sum and additional service is provided on a price by case basis.

- Purchasers have an incentive similar to that under block contracts when deciding how to fill places up to the initially agreed fixed volume. Providers have an incentive to overstate the complexity of the care service on the price by case part of the contract.

- The provider is guaranteed a certain income; however he must have enough capacity for the maximum number of referrals irrespective of the number of clients that are actually referred. Providers will be at risk financially if SSDs try to include their most costly clients under the fixed volume part of the contract.

Block and price by case contracts can be considered to be at opposite ends of a range of possible purchasing arrangements, with cost and volume contracts covering the intermediate range.

Block contracts may be more appropriate where it is easier to quantify inputs than number of cases. They tend to be the cheapest and easiest to negotiate. In such circumstances as residential care for elderly people, where a wide choice of providers already exists, or could be created, neither block contracts nor cost and volume contracts of a significant volume are desirable, since they tend to restrict competition. Where there is little competition, however, for example for services for specialised groups, a significant volume and timescale commitment may be necessary to ensure the provider's viability. Cost per case contracts are the most flexible and allow greatest choice. They are, however, likely to be more expensive to negotiate and to command a higher price since the provider takes the full risk on volume."

Note that the last sentence contains an explicit recognition by the Department of Health that risk is a legitimate cost to be reflected in the contract price.

Price and the contribution of volunteers

The time, skills and experience of volunteers are not assets which a voluntary organisation can commit to meet a contractual obligation as freely as those of its employees, or the equipment, vehicles or premises it owns.

The supply of suitable volunteers for a given service in a given area may vary. Some may wish to have a say in the work they take on. An organisation's complement of volunteers may well include individuals of different ability and productivity, a mix that may change during the life of the contract.

The uncertainty of these and other factors means that organisations supplying volunteer-intensive services should press for contracts which do not specify any fixed measure of service based on volunteer time, but merely specify the actions expected to lead to the hoped for service.

A parallel would be an advertising agency which does not guarantee additional sales from a campaign , nor does it suffer financial penalties if the campaign fails. If the purchaser is unhappy they have the option of not renewing the contract.

At the very least you may wish to seek some protection in the contract against the under-supply of volunteers. If the contract is priced by outputs you could well face a double bind: not enough volunteers means fewer units of service provision yielding less income at a time when you must spend more on supporting hard-pressed existing volunteers and recruiting new ones.

Organisations should be aware of the potential cost to quality of taking on – as a contract commitment – levels of work which can only be met by stretching resources of volunteer time and goodwill. Particular caution should be exercised where volunteers may feel under an obligation (to themselves or their clients) to do more work and cut down on say, training and expenses in order to reduce costs and thereby win a contract.

You will need to maintain your resolute commitment to quality above cost-efficiency and to good practice in volunteering throughout the process of contract negotiation – especially during haggling over price – and subsequently when you are providing the service under contract, and faced with real rather than projected costs.

Volunteers may be invaluable; but it is sometimes helpful to be able to put a value on their contribution, particularly in negotiation with purchasers of services. There are different ways of attaching a value to labour and services. You can begin by asking the pragmatic question "If no volunteers were available what would you have to pay people to carry out these tasks?" It may help to couch your answer in terms of minimum comparisons: find a job which is broadly or even partly similar.

For example "Part of what our volunteers do is like what care assistants do, but they do other things as well; so the time of three volunteers covering 18 hours a week between them can be valued as being worth at least £4,658 a year (half an £8,000 salary plus pension plus national insurance). In your Income and Expenditure budget you could then show an expenditure item of £4,586 (the value of the service given), matched by an income item of £4,586 (the value of the volunteer labour donated). It may be even appropriate to divide your volunteers contributions into minimum comparison bands, and total each band as a separate item.

There are no accounting conventions in general use for representing voluntary contributions of labour. But it may help to show them either in financial projections and balance sheets, or as an attached note.

Such valuations can produce surprising results. You cannot, of course use them to press the purchaser to give you that £4,586. But you can use them as a lever for other concessions, particularly if you are a monopoly supplier. You are adding a value to the service, which they as purchasers could not obtain except by spending more money.

Valuation of the contribution of voluntary management committees has already been considered under Indirect Costs. There is also a special category of volunteers whose contributions ought also be considered and costed appropriately – the many members of paid staff in voluntary organisations who carry out tasks and assume responsibilities far beyond their job descriptions and salaries. If this is a significant occurrence in your organisation then you seriously should consider separating the voluntary component out and valuing it separately from the costing of staff posts. This becomes essential if this is how your organisation maintains a quality service on inadequate funding.

Calculating a level of service for a given price

The contract specification calls for providing 500 units of service at the required quality level. You have calculated that it will cost your organisation £30,000 to do this, yielding a unit cost of £60.

The purchaser, who is operating within cash limits, informs you that regrettably there is only £20,000 available. At this point providers of service have a number of options:

- seeking other funding to provide 500 units at the required quality level – in effect subsidising the purchaser.
- provide 500 units but reducing the quality level

The first two options lie outside the scope if this book. Before you make your choice you should explore what the third option would mean:

- maintaining the quality level but reducing the number of Units

So, in our example what number of Units at the required quality level can you provide for £20,000?

It is clear from these two examples that the answer will depend on the balance between Fixed and Variable costs in your service:

How the calculation is done

From the figures for £30,000 we know that the Variable Unit Cost is £24. Subtract the Fixed Costs from the total price, and divide the remainder by the Variable Unit Cost.

i.e £20,000 – £18,000 = £2,000

£2,000/24 = 83.33.

Note: depending on what your Unit of service is you may have to round down to the nearest whole figure. Your offer to help one third of a client may not be appreciated.

What this means

- Where fixed costs are high and variable costs are low, as in Example A, then a reduction in price produces a disproportionately large drop in the level of service that can be provided – reducing the number of units from 500 to 83. Conversely an increase in price should – Break points permitting – produce a disproportionately large increase in service.

- Where fixed costs are low, and variable costs high, as in Example B, then cutting the price produces a smaller drop in service – down to 262. On the other hand increases in the level of service will be more expensive.

Figure 12.1a: FIXED AND VARIABLE COSTS

	Example A Higher fixed costs – lower variable costs		Example B: Lower fixed costs – higher variable costs	
Income target	£30,000	£20,000	£30,000	£20,000
(minus) total fixed costs	18,000	18,000	9,000	9,000
equals total variable costs	12,000	2,000	21,000	11,000
total	30,000	20,000	30,000	20,000
divided by no. of units	500	83	500	262
equals total unit cost	60	240	60	76
made up of a fixed unit cost	36	216	18	34
and a variable unit cost	24	24	42	42

Both these examples make two assumptions;

- that fixed costs remain fixed in spite of the substantial reduction in activity
- that variable costs vary in direct proportion to the volume of the service, no matter how high or low that volume is. These are assumptions you should question quite carefully in relation to your own costings.

Fixed costs can only be fixed for a given range. What that range is can only be discovered by a detailed and practical understanding of how the service is provided. You should pay particular attention to the break points in staff, supervision ratios, equipment, vehicles and premises.

Social care services are by definition labour intensive and any large scale cut in service volume is going to affect staff numbers. Where a range of activities requiring specialised staff are a required element of quality it may not be possible to reduce staff levels beyond a certain point. The same may be true of a range of facilities in a building.

For smaller organisations reductions in staff levels beyond a certain point may threaten the viability of the organisation, or its capacity to sustain a quality service. Small voluntary organisations provide some of the highest quality services, but they are also extremely vulnerable.

Consistency is an indispensable element of quality

In our example the size of the discrepancy between the costed figure you have produced and the available money is so great that you may have to re-calibrate the range of fixed costs. It is hard to see how any re-costing could avoid reducing staffing levels. This will have certain knock on effects which will require adjustments to costs other than simply salaries. Fewer staff may need:

- Less supervision, training and equipment;
- They travel less, make fewer phone calls and use fewer materials

Reductions in staffing costs do not necessarily have to be made by axing full-time posts. They may be made through part-time and seasonal working arrangements, or the use of sessional staff and freelances. These may produce marginal additional savings through reduced (or no) National Insurance and pension contributions, and incur some additional expenditure eg on training, (three half-timers may need more training than two full-timers) equipment, recruitment, etc.

Reducing the volume of service may well have consequences for your indirect costs, which we have hitherto thought of as being fixed. So they are but only for a given range. Having re-calibrated your fixed direct costs, indirect costs must follow suit. Take care in selecting your system of apportionment. Your formula should as far as possible reflect what would actually need to happen to maintain quality in the new circumstances of a smaller volume of service. Do ten volunteers and two staff delivering 250 units need only half the management and administrative backing of 20 volunteers and four staff delivering 500 units (assuming a direct correlation between staff numbers and units).

How variable costs may vary in relation to volume is again a matter of looking at what the costs are composed of. Variable costs tend to be made up of goods or services bought in; you may find that to buy less pushes up the unit price. Alternatively you could buy in larger quantities and hold larger stocks; what would this mean for your cash flow?

In supplying smaller volumes you will usually encounter some expenditure which cannot be reduced without prejudicing quality, for example the need to have a qualified member of staff on duty for a certain minimum number of hours per week.

At the other end of the spectrum you may encounter other limiting factors. Increasing volumes while maintaining quality may also present problems. There may be shortages of skilled staff, suitable volunteers, or available appropriate premises. It is dangerous to simply scale up Unit Costs – you may miss significant break points incurring extra expenditure or savings through economies of scale.

Negotiating aids

You should go into negotiation with a thorough knowledge of the costings that your organisation has done on the contract. As well as your Income & Expenditure Budget, it may be helpful to prepare some other costing briefs:

- You need to have an unambiguous written record of what your unit costs include – and what they do not.
- Bargaining tokens, and their value. What are you prepared to trade, and what will it cost you.? In order to answer these questions you must understand the break points in your activity and identify the limiting factors on your ranges of:
- Direct fixed costs
- Indirect costs
- Variable costs

and the Unit Costs that are calculated from them.

A costed brief for negotiation

Non-negotiable "bottom lines"

What is the minimum price you can accept without compromising fair terms and conditions for staff and volunteers, standards of service for users or other areas of organisation's work? You may for example calculate that you need a guaranteed income on a cost and volume contract of a least £17,000 in order to give security of employment to staff and an acceptable level of service to users.

A valuation of all the contributions to the cost of the service

- Price paid by purchasing authority
- Subsidy from other sources: grants, sponsorship, charitable donations in cash or in kind
- Contribution from volunteers
- Subsidy (=loss) from the provider organisation.

Price negotiation may well be focused on how you have calculated indirect costs. You will find it easiest to defend your position if the allocation of central costs reflects the reality.

Figure 12.2: EXAMPLE OF A COSTED BRIEF FOR NEGOTIATION

Salary Scp 24	7,015
National Insurance	733
Pension	351
Redundancy fund	7
Total salary costs	**8,610**
Staff training	500
Travel	350
Marginal increases	300
Total cost	**9,256**
Total	

Additional units provided: 120.

Reduction in unit cost: £1.35.

But for each 1.5 additional staff or more, add £12,500 for extra management and admin.

£9,256 x 3 + £12,500 = £40,266.

Additional units provided: 360.

Reduction in unit cost: £0.90.

You may need to be discreet in the presentation of figures. If you don't want to call attention to an item of expenditure, put it about two thirds of the way down the list. Find an innocuous name for it. Or lump it together with a larger more acceptable item.

Morag sent her sheet of costings with a brief letter to Dr. Anderson, who in turn suggested she drop by for a chat. Her first move was to return the sheet to Morag, saying never to reveal that it had been sent in the first place. The costing, she said was fine; the scheme appeared, in NHS treatment terms, amazingly cost-effective. The idea of achieving substantial results at a cost of only £135 a child was a dream, when compared with the cost of the various professional therapies normally suggested for such children. But any contract would have to go through her Practice Manager and there was no way he would allow £1,000 for evaluation to go through on a 'preventive treatment' budget. This amount would have to go under a general heading 'administration' which would include not just a third of the total salary bill but more like 40% – and this could be justified by saying the developing a new project was more time-consuming than merely continuing an existing one. And anyway there was no advantage in presenting existing project costs until asked to justify those for the new development – which might never happen.

So Morag re-drafted, and submitted a formal proposal. This stated that the Munster Project would do, what it would cost, and that the agreement could be terminated by either party at any time subject the completion of, and payment for, any clubs already formed and into their ten-week cycle. She suggested that a simple exchange of this letter and of a note of acceptance from the practice would constitute an entirely adequate contract. In this she was advised by her husband, a solicitor, who said an agreement was an agreement and no amount of fine or complicated wording would make it more or less legal.

When the practice group meeting considered Morag's proposal, the practice manager reported that they could cover a substantial part of the cost from sessional clinic payments, and the balance out of the budget the practice had put aside specifically for the development of work promoting the mental health of children. Dr. Anderson won support for her view that the programme would be an exciting and highly cost-effective innovation, especially when considering the expensive alternatives which would otherwise almost certainly be needed by at least some of these children.

But one partner, Dr. Low, and he unfortunately the most senior in years and status, objected strongly; this project, he said, just consists of volunteers giving some admittedly hard-done-by children a nice time. It was ridiculous, he said, to spend substantial money on this, money which could otherwise be used for serious medicine. Having effectively a veto on his colleagues, this might have been the end of it. But Dr. Anderson suggested she would consult with Morag and see if £1,000 could not be saved by careful examination of the costings. If so, would not Dr. Low go along with his younger colleagues? Sensing that he was in a minority, he assented.

When told, Morag was not surprised; it had all sounded too good to be true. She mentally cut down her contribution to the evaluation by £500, which she already know the Poly would accept, and mentally prepared to raise the other £500 from the so far untapped local charities of New Southtown. She sent a revised proposal letter and got her contract.

(Continued on Page 186)

Chapter 13
Managing a Contract

As we noted in the Introduction it is during the financial management of a contract that you will find out how good your earlier costing work has been. You should of course be carrying out financial management for your whole organisation – not just the contracted service. In fact it will be impossible to consider the financial performance of the contract service without reference to the performance of the rest of the organisation, as this will have a considerable influence through, for example, the level of indirect costs or cash flow.

Financial management is a tool that can be used to understand and control the finances of the organisation, so that its resources can be directed towards securing policy objectives. It offers a means of keeping individual cost centres within budget. It collects facts for use in future budgeting and costing. It supplies information for wider management decisions and future planning.

Many people dislike financial management because they associate it with crude budgetary control, a tool for cutting costs, reducing services, wages and staffing levels. People in voluntary organisations and elsewhere are also reluctant to use administrative systems which offer them no incentives – better working conditions or more resources for example. Getting them to submit information without also involving them in correlation and review invites non-cooperation, or poor co-operation, yielding untrustworthy figures.

Many voluntary organisations have got by with an informal approach to financial management, based on the "feel" of staff or the management committee, built up over several years of experience. Taking on a contract may well introduce new patterns of financial activity into your organisation which will need to understood and controlled. Care should be taken to produce a system which is thorough and comprehensive, but which can be operated efficiently and in a reasonable time. This is not an easy balance to strike. It is obviously better to spend 1 day a month establishing that you are losing between £2,000 and £3,000 a month and have some time to do something about it, than to spend five days a month establishing that last month's loss was actually 2,789.87p. On the other hand you do need to be sure that you have counted all items of expenditure; having raised your supplementary £3,000 you will not wish to discover that the shortfall is actually £6,000.

Most of the work of financial management is in the early stages of setting up a system, and in learning to operate it. After the first few months – and certainly after the first year it will become more routine.

Financial management means integrating six activities:

- Planning – producing budgets and projections
- Recording actual transactions in your book-keeping system
- Preparing regular reports -"management accounts" – from the books
- Reviewing performance by comparing reports and budgets.
- Revising plans in the light of performance review, changing circumstances and other management decisions
- Taking corrective action

You should seek the advice and help of your accountant in establishing the appropriate financial management system for your organisation. Consultation with the book-keeper is important too; their help in preparing management accounts will be invaluable.

Planning

We have looked in detail in earlier chapters at the process of planning. In small organisations the financial parts will often be on your mind all the time. In bigger organisations you will need to undertake major financial planning for all your organisation's work at least annually, in order to draw up an annual budget. In practice this can be a very extended process. You may need to make major revisions during the year, as events unfold – the failure of a major grant to materialise, higher than anticipated demand and so on.

For the contracted service your plan is the contract itself, together with the specification and other ancillary documents, and the costed financial projections we have looked at earlier in this book.

Recording actual transactions in your book-keeping system

So far in this book we have been mainly concerned with invented, projected figures. You must now deal with the actual payments and receipts. Just as we have been trying to anticipate all the possible items of expenditure and income, so you must now ensure that all actual items of income and expenditure are represented in your accounts.

You should take advice from your accountant and book-keeper before fiddling around with your book-keeping system. If taking on a contract means a substantial increase in turnover, and in complexity of internal transactions, or the use of credit you will probably need to switch to a double-entry book-keeping system if you are not already using one.

Plainly it will simplify matters if planning, recording and

reporting are all done using a common structure of cost centres and classes. You need to be sure that the range of "pigeonholes" that they create will cater for all the kinds of income and expenditure you will be incurring. You may need to make new distinctions, and introduce new cost centres and classes. You may wish to group them differently. If you are considering these changes remember that inventing new classes half-way through an accounting period will create muddle, errors, and possible losses. Only do so at the start of a new financial year. Furthermore in changing the structure of your accounting system you may destroy the basis for making comparisons with the past, and so lose a useful yardstick. You will also have to ensure that the book-keeper, and everyone who authorises expenditure gets written notice of the changes, and training in the new systems, if necessary.

Preparing regular reports from the books

It is no good waiting until the contract is about to expire to discover that your plan started to go off the rails 10 months ago.

You will need to prepare, at regular intervals, a set of reports that describe key aspects of the finances of the organisation. These are often known as management reports or management accounts. The reports should warn you of departures from the key elements of your plan: the projections you have made for your Income and Expenditure account, and for cash flow. As a minimum you will need to produce monthly reports on these.

Monthly Income and Expenditure reports

The monthly Income and Expenditure report - figure 13.1 – lists classes of Expenditure and Income in rows. Each cost centre has 4 columns;

Column (a) shows the Actual figure for the month – the total from the books; Column (b) shows the Actual figures for the

Figure 13.1: MONTHLY INCOME AND EXPENDITURE REPORT

Income and expenditure report June 1993

Cost Centre : 02 Day centre   Contract: Loamshire "B"
Printed: 22.7.93

	(a)	(b)	(c)	(c) - (b)
	Actual this month	**Actual year to date**	**Budget year to date**	**Variance**
Expenditure				
Capital	0	7,500	10,000	2,500
Revenue				
Set up costs	470	3,630	3,830	200
Direct costs - fixed				
Total salaries	2,597	7,794	7,985	191
Staff training	225	250	125	(125)
Staff travel	26	87	62	(25)
Rent	0	375	437	62
Rates	0	0	0	0
Electricity	35	35	62	27
Gas	62	62	87	25
Water	73	73	37	(35)
Repair & maintenance	0	0	37	37
Telephone	195	195	125	(70)
Postage	0	25	12	(12)
Stationery	9	37	19	(18)
Photocopying	15	34	12	(21)
Depreciation	417	417	417	(0)
Total direct fixed costs	**3,654**	**9,384**	**9,421**	**37**

	Actual this month	Actual year to date	Budget year to date	Variance
Infirect costs				
Management & Admin.	2,254	2,254	2,254	0
Insurance	350	350	87	(262)
Bank interest	0	0	142	142
Total indirect costs	**2,604**	**2,604**	**2,484**	**(120)**
Total fixed costs	**6,736**	**15,618**	**15,735**	**117**
Variable costs				
Catering supplies	180	727	750	23
Gas	0	0	75	75
Water	0	0	8	8
Total variable costs	**180**	**727**	**832**	**105**
Total revenue expenditure	**6,916**	**16,345**	**16,567**	**222**
Income				
Loamshire "B"	16,500	16,500	16,473	(26)
Sales	40	90	94	3
Total	**16,540**	**16,590**	**16,567**	**(23)**
BALANCE	9,624	245	0	(245)

Year to date – i.e. column (a) added to Column (b) in last months report.

Column (c) shows the projected figure for the year to date from the budget; (a calculation much more speedily undertaken on a spreadsheet) and Column (d) shows the difference between the Columns (b) and (c) (in accounting terms called the Variance).

The actual figures in Columns (a) and (b) should be adjusted to include all the payments and receipts due for the period in question – regardless of whether the transaction has actually taken place yet. They should also not include any relating to other periods; i.e. no payments relating to next month, or in the case of Column (a), relating to 2 months ago.

Prepayments and accruals

Prepayments and accruals are a way of adjusting actual figures for a given period so that they reflect all the income and expenditure related to it. For example telephone charges:

- The rental you pay on your system and apparatus is in made in advance – a prepayment
- The charges you pay for calls are in arrears – accruals

You should also split the VAT accordingly.

So in the month of January it may be that no telephone bill was received or paid, but the adjusted accounts should show:

- As prepayments - one third of the advance payment for rental of equipment plus VAT from the preceding bill
- As accruals - one third of the payment in arrears for calls plus VAT from the next bill

Cash Flow

The second kind of report you need to make is on your organisation's cash flow. You need to adapt the Cash Flow Forecast you made earlier (as we have adapted the Income and Expenditure budget) by introducing additional columns for the actual figures, as shown in figure 13.2a.

Remember that cash flow is about when money enters or leaves your organisation or its bank accounts. Internal transactions between cost centres do not count. Nor do adjusted accruals; but actual payments (including prepayments) and receipts do. So to get your totals of income and expenditure you must go back to the books. Your Monthly I&E reports could be very misleading.

If you have spent more or received less than projected in the first month then you will carry forward a smaller surplus or larger deficit to the second month, and you will have to recalculate all your figures for subsequent months.

Figure 13.2 : BUDGET FILLED IN – ACTUAL BLANK
Careless Trust rolling cash flow forecast

	APRIL BUDGET	APRIL ACTUAL	MAY BUDGET	MAY ACTUAL		YEAR TOTALS BUDGET
Income	11,000	Ø	Ø	Ø		**44,000**
Less expenditure	5,500	Ø	3,500	Ø		**44,000**
Plus carried forward	Ø		5,500	Ø		**Ø**
Surplus (Deficit)	5,500	Ø	2,000	Ø		**Ø**

Scope and frequency of reports

Morag does not need many written reports. If she checks that her grants and payments were as planned, and that she does not overspend on any of her club, she is unlikely to go far wrong.

If you have a high proportion of variable costs, and/or are providing a service which is subject to large fluctuations in volume you may need to produce management accounts more frequently. It may be possible to identify one or two key classes of expenditure which lead or determine the rest of variable costs, and prepare say weekly reports on those alone.

Or it may be that you need to find indicators of rising expenditure or falling income that will react more quickly than your accounting system – weekly or daily reports from supervisors, attendance registers or logs which can be scrutinised daily. The costs of two busy weeks at the start of the month may not appear in the management reports at the start of the following month, or even the month after as raising invoices, expenses claims from staff, petty cash reimbursements etc may take time to enter the books and emerge in reports.

Even if your variable costs are relatively low, or you are providing an even level of service you will still want to concentrate your attention on the larger items in the report which will have a more serious impact on both the surplus or deficit you incur, or on the cash flow.

In addition to these management accounts it is also advisable to have some regular management scrutiny of the books themselves – rather than the reports – to ensure that Expenditure and Income have been correctly classified and set against the correct cost centres, in the right proportions. This should be done soon after the introduction of a new system, or of new cost centres and classes, and then at regular if less frequent intervals thereafter – perhaps quarterly. If errors are found then a list of correcting transfers should be made so that subsequent reports are accurate.

Reviewing performance by comparing reports and budgets

The Income and Expenditure report
Analysing this report does not mean simply checking whether the Grand Total in the bottom right hand corner

shows a surplus or a deficit. You need to undertake an Analysis of Variances. This involves satisfying yourself that you understand every discrepancy between the actual and the budgeted figures.

Examine the report line by line and ask yourself – or colleagues:

• What do actual figures in Columns (a) and (b) include?

• What do they not include?

Pay particular attention to items of expenditure which are paid at quarterly or longer intervals – bills for telephone, gas & electricity; water rates, rent, etc. You need to be quite clear that prepayments and accruals are fully and accurately apportioned to the period under scrutiny.

Then, turn your attention to internal transfers. It may not be practical to calculate contributions due from "user" cost centres more frequently than once a quarter. You need to be sure up to what point such charges have been "posted".

Cash flow report

While it is possible to consider the Income and Expenditure Account reports for different cost centres separately, so far as cash flow is concerned your organisation's needs must be considered as a whole. Since cash flow is partly derived from the Income and Expenditure account it follows that an organisation running several different cost centres needs to co-ordinate its reviews, so that a comprehensive assessment of cash flow can be quickly made. Quickly because undetected and unforeseen cash flow deficits can be very expensive.

Your Cash Flow Report will exclude internal transactions, and accruals but include prepayments. If it shows an unanticipated deficit, or a larger than anticipated deficit then you need to take immediate action to find the necessary cash to float your operation. Even if it merely shows a smaller than anticipated surplus you should still mount enquiries to see where the actual figures differ from the projected. If it is just because you made a payment earlier than anticipated ask yourself if the same will happen in any other classes, and comfort yourself with the knowledge that your cash flow later in the year will be that much easier.

If however the extra deficit or smaller surplus is due to a payment or payments made at a higher level or in addition to those projected then you must anticipate a progressive worsening of your cash flow, and take steps accordingly.

You will have to revise your rolling cashflow forecast in the light of the actual report. However since the next step in the financial management process may also call for revisions to both the I&E account and therefore to the cashflow requirement leave revising your cash flow forecast until it is completed.

Cash Flow Report – an example

Let us look at our old friends at the Careless Trust.

Figure 13.3: ACTUAL FILLED IN
Careless Trust Rolling cash flow forecast

	APRIL BUDGET	APRIL ACTUAL	MAY BUDGET	JUNE BUDGET		YEAR TOTALS BUDGET
Income	11,000	7,000	0	0		51,000
Less expenditure	5,500	6,000	3,500	3,500		50,000
Plus carried forward			1,000	1,000		1,000
Surplus (Deficit)	5,500	1,000	2,500	2,500		1,000

At the end of April they look at their books and discover that instead of receiving the forecast amount of £11,000, they only received £7,000. And they spent £6,000 rather than the forecast £5,500. Putting these figures into the APRIL ACTUAL column they find that they carry forward to May only £1,000, instead of the forecast £5,500 (see Figure 13.2a above MAY BUDGET column). So they can now adjust the MAY BUDGET column, and because of the knock-on effect of the Carried forward row, they must also adjust the BUDGET columns for the rest of the year. This now yields higher deficits (up to £2,500) and in more months (8), starting with May. Given that it is already May, prompt action will be necessary.

So the Trust must now:

- Make arrangements to finance these deficits,
- Work any costs of borrowing into a revised Income and Expenditure Budget
- Revise the rolling cash flow forecast again to take account of Income and Expenditure Budget revisions.

Revising plans in the light of performance review, changing circumstances and other management decisions

Having thus understood what the Income and Expenditure report represents you should then review the accuracy of your projected costings. It is worth doing this line by line, marking as appropriate items which need

- no action - √
- attention now – X
- review again next month – ?

Particularly in the first months of a contract it may not be possible to get a clear indication of how accurate your estimates have been. However hopefully by the end of the first quarter – and definitely by the end of the second quarter you should know where (if anywhere) the problems lie.

Problems usually come not singly but in combinations. They may produce compounded results which may cancel each other out in the short term but if untreated could produce serious difficulties later. You can classify problems in your Income and Expenditure report according to this scheme:

Expenditure

- Estimate unrealistically low
- Estimate satisfactory but actual spending higher than necessary.

Income

- Estimate unrealistically high
- Estimate satisfactory but failure to earn full potential.

Before you move to finding a solution you need to correlate the financial reports on the service with other reports on the provision of the service. The Income and Expenditure report gives a picture of the actual finances of the service; you will want to verify how closely that actuality matches the projected service in terms of quantity and quality, changes in client need, strain on staff, etc.

The quantitative correlation is easier, provided that you have adopted appropriate measures of output to measure as Unit Costs. You will simply calculate your actual Unit Costs (from the actual costs divided by the actual number of units provided) for comparisons with your projections. It may be more helpful to make separate calculations for Fixed Direct Unit Costs, Indirect Unit Costs and Variable Unit Costs. This kind of simple calculation and comparison can provide vital early warnings of problems, particularly if you anticipate substantial increases in the volume of service later on.

You need information from service delivery staff, volunteers and supervisors to see if the break points actually do occur when and where and how you thought they would.

USING UNIT COSTS – an example

The Cold Harbour Association has contracted to provide up to 600 units of service with the Kiplington District Council, to be paid for on a price by case based on projected Total Unit Costs of £7.50. The maximum value of the contract is therefore 600 x £7.50 = £4,500.

Two months into the contract the treasurer adjusts and reviews her financial reports and sees that actual expenditure for the two month period totals £400. But reports from the service Co-ordinator show that only 50 units have been provided, yielding a Unit Cost of £8.00. The treasurer calculates that the Association has in effect already lost 50p on each of 50 units = £25.00. Furthermore she calculates that unless corrective action is taken to reduce actual Unit Costs the Association stands to run up a deficit of £300 (50p on each of 600 units) by the end of the contract.

Correlation of financial reports with qualitative reports is harder because of the indirect and complex relationship between finance and quality. You can begin by looking at the quality factors identified earlier, and seeing if they are in place and operating as planned, and costing what you thought. You may find that in practice some procedures or resources designed to ensure quality are in fact redundant.

If you are encountering difficulties in maintaining quality it is useful to know where (if anywhere) there are unused resources that could be redeployed. An underspent publicity budget could be reallocated to increase staff training. Lower than anticipated Unit Costs in Contract A could give you the option of reducing the volume (while maintaining projected income) and redeploying some staff to hard pressed Contract B.

Lastly you may need to revise your plans to take into account external factors like a change in interest rates, and management decisions like investing more heavily in a contract you expect to renew on a larger scale.

A new budget and a new cash flow forecast

You will need to draw up a new Income and Expenditure budget, ensuring that:

- Your assumptions are fully revised and re-written as appropriate
- All consequences for other cost centres and longer term projections are fully worked through

Revising the Income and Expenditure budget for an individual cost centre will probably affect several other cost centres. If your revised budgets call for higher expenditure there will almost certainly be a short term worsening of your cash flow. Even though there may be no net change in the overall value of the revised budget there may still be consequences for the organisation's cash flow; some payments may be brought forward, some receipts put back.

So you will also need to draw up a new rolling cash flow forecast, based on:

- The new Income and Expenditure budgets
- The latest actual information available on the actual surpluses or deficits carried forward
- Any changes in interest rates or borrowing conditions

You must also decide what to do with any new cash surpluses than may be (temporarily!) created.

Taking corrective action

Having understood the nature of a problem you can apply an appropriate solution. If you have multiple problems you will need a combination of measures to tackle them. You have a number of options:

- You can simply reduce expenditure in the offending class where an overspend has occurred;
- You can revise your costings by re-allocating a surplus

from another class or cost centre which is underspent (or is lower priority and can be cut) to an overspent one, without any net increase in the whole budget. This is known as net. While organisations are free to transfer allocations between their Income/Expenditure classes within a cost centre, they may find it less easy to do so between cost centres, particularly if they relate to separate contracts with different purchasing authorities.

- You can revise your costings by increasing the allocation to the overspent class or cost centre, and thereby increasing the value of the whole budget. This means getting more income.

- You can try to renegotiate the price of the contract, either from now or (less likely) retrospectively.

FUNNY MONEY: SLUSH, SLIPPAGE AND END OF YEAR UNDERSPENDS

A slush fund may be no more than an organisation's reserves or contingency fund. It must be properly accounted for; and form part of the audited accounts. You may not however, wish to draw its existence, or size, to the attention of a purchasing authority.

Slippage is a term used by some people to describe minor underspends in cost centres and/or classes of expenditure, which when taken altogether can produce a significant sum. Slippage in expenditure can only be used if you are sure that there is no slippage in income, and towards the end of the year when the final size of any underspend becomes clear.

As the end of the financial year – or the end of a contract approaches you may find it in your organisation's interest to spend up all your budget. If a purchaser – or other funder – sees unspent monies they may try to reduce the next contract price or grant accordingly. How far they succeed will depend on many factors. But it may well be prudent and helpful for your organisation to turn cash surpluses from a contract into assets or services which while contributing to your contract service also benefit your non-contract activities.

You also need to ensure that decisions are actually implemented by people in your organisation. Remember that budgets only describe a state of affairs: altering a column of figures by itself won't save you a penny. Depending on the pricing mechanism contained in your contract you may need to act quickly to either control costs, or increase volume and income.

Regardless of how your contract is priced it cannot be emphasised too strongly that early and prompt action to adjust your plan if it is going wrong will save your organisation a lot of time, anguish and money. No deficit was ever diminished by delay.

You may need to take action to cut costs. This is never easy. But it will prove less difficult if you have already had wide involvement in financial planning and management from staff, volunteers and management committee members.

Checklist

Setting up a system:
- Consultation
- Appropriate cost centres and classes
- Income and Expenditure and Cash flow report frequency
- Scrutiny of books

Regular reports:
- Income and Expenditure: Analysis of variances
- Check cash flow
- Check accuracy of costings
- Calculate actual Unit Costs
- Correlate with Quality reports, Other Management decisions, External factors.

Morag >> *a continuing story* (from Page 168)

Three years later, things were much changed. Morag's salary grant from the Council had been cut and she was being required to pay a full rent for her office. On the other hand she had signed three further contracts with different parts of the NHS and one with the local probation service. She was still running clubs for ten of her original schools but they were now paying the modest costs out of that part of the LMS budgets allocated for children with special needs. She had a full time assistant and was looking forward to expanding the project and her time with it as her youngest child started school. And she had a file of costings prepared for different proposals and contracts, backed by one sacrosanct folder headed "The Truth". She had got to grips with the idea that each new project affected all the others, and that, as she was organised at present, she could only cope with pricing a complete 'club'; but what should she do about the people now asking for a price per child, without being able to guarantee the number of children there would be?

And now the County Social Services was asking her to provide costings for a county-wide prevention service. Morag realised that the back-of-an-envelope calculations that had served her so well until now would no longer do. Was there a book that would lead her into a more detailed and thorough approach?

Appendix 1
Checking for Errors

You will need to check your figures to make sure that the numbers before you are correct. You should begin by checking your own calculations. This is best undertaken at the start of a new session of work, as a way of up-dating yourself on where you have got to. You should a carry out your final checks as a separate exercise.

If large sums are involved you should also have them checked by someone else who has not been closely involved in the costing exercise. A fresh eye will spot errors to which you have become blind through over familiarity.

There are four categories of error for which you should be looking:

1. Incorrect assumptions

A useful technique is to tell the story back from the figures in front of you. Take each costing line and ask yourself – or have a partner ask you – what assumptions it is based on.

When you've done that check again for consistency among assumptions. Do the numbers of staff you have allowed for tally with the training and travel allowances?

Beware of inheriting assumptions that are no longer appropriate from earlier drafts e.g. about vacancy rates, likely pay awards.

When formulae are repeated in different cost centres or

classes or years be particularly careful to ensure that they are correctly applied, and appropriately modified to cater for different circumstances.

2. Omissions

Have you actually costed everything?

Talk yourself – or a partner – through the delivery of the service; who will do what, when, where and how. Ask service delivery staff.

Indirect costs: review all your organisation's staff and their activities and ask yourself – or a partner – what they contribute to the contracted service.

Check that internal trading between cost centres is accurately and completely recorded; that debits from cost centre A appear as receipts to the same value in cost centre B.

3. Arithmetical errors

Many of these may be detected by use of the balancing box, i.e. the totals along the bottom and down the right hand side should add up to the same.

4. Transposition errors

When figures are copied by hand, or re-keyed then there is always a chance that a number may be missed off the beginning, or added to the end, or two middle numbers reversed – with obvious consequences. The quickest method to find out whether there are any errors is to re-total all the copied numbers; the surest method of finding where the error occurs is to have someone to read out the copied figures as you check them against the original.

Appendix 2
Using Computers

Computers can help with your financial planning and control by enabling you to undertake much more complex and detailed financial calculations in a fraction of the time of either mental arithmetic or a calculator. This will be of particular benefit when you have to:

- Rehearse a range of options,
- Use a large number of classes of expenditure
- Project costs over several years
- Distribute costs between several cost centres
- Trade between cost centres
- Revise frequently in the light of actual performance to date

It follows that such a system will be more useful in the pricing and negotiation stage when rapid re-calculations may be required, and during the implementation of the contract, when close financial control is necessary.

There are two kinds of software which can help. Firstly there are spreadsheets, which do nothing more than enable your computer to act as a super-calculator.

Secondly there are the integrated accounts packages which allow the user to carry out full double-entry book-keeping, and use the information so recorded in making financial projections about the future. These have been considered too expensive to buy and install to be cost-effective for most small to medium sized groups.

Until recently smaller voluntary organisations were often advised to stick to their manual book-keeping systems. The only cost effective use of a computer might be a spreadsheet programme on which to make financial projections. Though some ingenious book-keepers have succeeded in adopting spreadsheets to make simple cash book financial records, they cannot be considered as a cost-effective full accounting system for most groups. That advice now needs to be reviewed as smaller organisations' accounting and budgeting needs become more complex, and as more powerful hardware and user-friendly software packages become available at lower prices.

Most organisations running integrated packages go for an IBM-compatible business PC (Personal Computer) and a dot-matrix or laser printer. Talk to your accountant about the most appropriate software package for your needs. Most accounts packages are sold as bundles of modules (hence package) which carry out different functions (e.g. payroll, purchase ledger).

A Sage Accounts package used by some smaller organisations could cost around £600; while a mid-range system like Multisoft will require detailed tailoring to your needs and support on installation and could cost £2,000 or more.

Spreadsheet programmes on their own are very much cheaper, but of course you will need to invest the time in setting up the framework and entering the formulae necessary to make the calculations you want. On simpler exercises you will find a calculator, pencil and rubber faster. You will in any case need to plan a spreadsheet on paper, where it is easier to see the main elements and broad categories; on a computer it is all too easy to lose track of what you are calculating.

Spreadsheet programmes do not provide much space for the words you need to explain the numbers. Clear recording of the assumptions on which a given spreadsheet is based, and disciplined and systematic housekeeping of files is important.

Checking that your programme actually does calculate the inter-relationships between cost centres that you think it does can take some time but is essential. It is advisable to carry out your checks on print-outs, rather than on-screen. You should not be looking at the arithmetic but at what the figures produced mean. Formulae which have been copied inadvertently or without appropriate modifications are a major source of error.

Every organisation's accounting needs differ, and you should take advice before embarking on computerisation. You are strongly recommended to take that advice from an accountant with some experience of using computers, rather than from a computer expert with some experience of accounts.

Beware of making the assumption that you should "get a computer to do the accounts". You – or someone in your organisation will have to use the computer to do the accounts. The benefit you derive from the figures the system produces will depend on the extent to which you understand how they are produced.

If you are going to install an integrated system, or just use a spreadsheet then it is a good idea to do so in advance of negotiating important contracts. Computerised accounts can undoubtedly save a great deal of time and many mistakes – but only if you are practised in their use. Setting up – and learning how to use them can be very time consuming, and a single slip, which may be very difficult to detect, can generate expensive errors.

You must also consider the position of your book-keeper, and your accountant if you have such colleagues (you may well do both jobs yourself). A positive attitude from both of them towards changing to a computerised system is essential. Day to day financial management in many voluntary organisations is in the hands of volunteers, often retired professionals who may well find unfamiliar new technology to be a threat. Any change may need to be handled with tact. Or you may be faced with changing your book-keeper, accountant as well as your financial systems, a treble step that is not to be taken lightly.

This book was written on an Amstrad PCW 8512, and the examples were prepared using the Mini-Office Spreadsheet programme. Both hardware and software could be bought for less than £500 (1992 price, inclusive of VAT).